NO 1 MORE
Hamster Wheel
RELATIONSHIPS
for Women

A Step by Step Process to Transform Unfulfilling Relationship Patterns

Louise VN Liebenberg

Hamster Wheel Relationships for Women. A Step by Step Process to Transform Unfulfilling Relationship Patterns. Accompanied by Stepping Off – The Hamster Wheel Workbook/ Louise VN Liebenberg — 1st edition.

Although the author and publisher have made every effort to ensure that the information in this book was correct at press time, the author and publisher don't assume and hereby disclaim any liability to any party for any loss, damage, or disruption caused by errors or omissions, whether such errors or omissions result from negligence, accident, or any other cause.

Adherence to all applicable laws and regulations, including international, federal, state and local governing professional licensing, business practices, advertising, and all other aspects of doing business in the US, Canada or any other jurisdiction is the sole responsibility of the reader and consumer.

DISCLAIMER

Neither the author nor the publisher assumes any responsibility or liability whatsoever on behalf of the consumer or reader of this material. Any perceived slight of any individual or organization is purely unintentional.

The resources in this book are provided for informational purposes only, and should not be used to replace the specialized training and professional judgment of a health care or mental health care professional.

Neither the author nor the publisher can be held responsible for the use of the information provided within this book. Please always consult a trained professional before making any decision regarding treatment of yourself or others.

The participants featured in this book have granted legal permission for the inclusion of their story. Some names and identifying details have been changed to protect the privacy of individuals.

Real!! Powerful, intriguing and true!

This book blew my mind as I began to read it. To see how it all starts, what I can do differently and how I can have the life I truly deserve all so succinctly outlined in the book as well as the workbook. Now that is powerful!

The lessons are so simple, yet so powerful all encompassed within the real life stories of women who sabotaged their lives one way or the other through not dealing with the causes, having damaging behaviors in their relationships, experiencing the negative symptoms and more importantly, not realizing that they held the key to their own loving relationships by understanding themselves and their patterns.

We're all on a journey called life, with very few tools or coping mechanisms to guide us through the traumas, emotional distress, hurts and programming of our belief systems. We follow blindly the path we THINK we've to, without realizing that the majority of the time we actually needed to change direction to get to the place we truly deserve. I say this, because my very own journey led me on a healing path that could only happen with the insight, guidance and thoughtfulness of experienced people who understand the depth of the mind, subconscious belief systems and the stagnant behaviors ingrained in my everyday life. I needed clear insights and absolute truth to move my thinking.

This incredible book is a must read for any woman who seeks mindfulness in her relationship. One that teaches resilience, perseverance, thoughtfulness, affirmations, self-care practices and worthiness. Transform your life by changing your thought patterns and setting healthy boundaries – guilt free!

I can guarantee that when you're done, you'll have the best outlook for a stunning life where you deserve the best and never settle for less ever again!! You'll feel honoured, valued and respected for the beautiful Soul that you are and I know for a fact, that Louise VN Liebenberg has found the winning formula to help you take your life to the next level. It's your CHOICE – always has been!

Arthie Moore – Founder of Ki Leadership Institute Pty Ltd.

I used to love watching the cute little hamsters running in their wheels at the pet shops. But it also made me sad. These little critters gave it their all, but never got anywhere, things never changed; they just got tired, stopped and then started again achieving the same disappointing result.

Are you a relationship hamster, repeating the same mistakes, feeling unfulfilled, stuck or resistant to change? If so, don't give up for there is a light at the end of the tunnel. That light is Life Skills Coach, Louise VN Liebenberg's new book... one that I highly recommend.

Louise writes with love and understanding, sharing personal stories of her own journey to help identify those negative patterns while offering tools for change, accepting your own responsibility and embracing self-empowerment.

These are the tools and techniques I use in my coaching practice. Now they are presented in a simple and powerful way. Hamster Wheel Relationships for Women is a valuable resource for women of all ages.

Cathy Brown – Master Law of Attraction Life Coach,
best-selling author of ACT: Align-Connect-Transform
https://lifecoachingbycathy.com/

Most people muddle through life from one knee-jerk reaction to the next. Sometimes one copes and sometimes not. Sometimes one gets it right and sometimes one doesn't. A hit or miss life.

For most it's about surviving the difficulties whilst searching for elusive happiness.

Hamster Wheel Relationships for Women provides a sound opportunity for one to stop and look deeply into those limiting coping mechanisms blindly adopted during one's informative years that have left one compromised in dealing with present daily challenges.

Through the use of the book and workbook, one can identify where these core limiting beliefs and coping skills began, and take the opportunity to take the first steps to overcoming and replacing them.

Louise's heart-opening accounts of her own painful journey are peppered throughout the book. Her vulnerability gives one permission to feel safe in stepping into one's own fragility without judgment.

Jenetta Barry – International Speaker and Founder of *The Epiphany Process - Creating new ways* of thinking and lasting new behaviors

Dedication

With much love and appreciation, I dedicate this book to you; braves ones, determined ones, who walked this walk with me.

And to the cats that keep my feet and my heart warm while I write at 5 am – Muffin, Zoli, Smokey and Steve the Elder.

Your task is not to seek for love, but merely to seek and find all the barriers within yourself that you have built against it.

– Rumi

Contents

I wrote this book for the desperate me from 12 years ago, who didn't know what else to try, where to get help and indeed that there was another way to happiness. Now I know that it's possible to change your life from the inside out, that great relationships do exist, that they look different than I thought, and that all I needed was better information.

Who's this book for?

This book is not only for women or singles. This book is for anyone trapped in a relationship in which they feel lonely, unheard and without support. (Yes, men can benefit from it too.)

This is a book for anyone struggling to retain connection and acceptance within relationships. It's for anyone who's finding it hard to voice their wants and needs within a relationship.

We can tumble from relationship to relationship and eventually find out we're repeating one key mistake. This book will help you identify that key mistake.

Or you could be in a long, dysfunctional relationship, based on repeating the same cycle over and over. This book will help you decipher and decode what the root cause is.

You'll love this book if you're tired of being on the Hamster Wheel of repeating the same relationship patterns and arguments – over and over.

(Please note that although for simplicity's sake I refer to 'him', these same markers, tools and reactions apply to those in same sex relationships.)

A NOTE OF CAUTION

You're going to find out things about yourself and relationships that may make you feel like you need to walk out of the (relationship) door this minute, or you may lay down super-big boundaries such as "Do this or the relationship is over". **I urge you to not make any big changes for the next six months**, or at least until you get to the end of this book!

I am not an advocate of summarily giving up on relationships because:

- I believe most relationships can not only be saved but can be improved and be happy.

- We need our dysfunctional current relationship to learn healthy patterns. When we don't learn better tools in our current relationship, we just repeat the pattern with the next partner.

- When we change our own outlook, behavior and coping tools, those around us change in response to our healthier ways. I know it sounds improbable but trust me on this – I have seen it happen over and over in the lives of the women who tried this process and changed their own behaviors!

- Abusive relationships where your life and health are at stake don't fall into this category. Get professional help and support as soon as possible!

We often have these set beliefs:

I Have to Fix This
I Cannot Ask for Help
I Trust Only Myself to Get Things Done

If you're reading this, you most likely fall into this category. If this sounds like you I want to assure you that I know about the long, hard and lonely road of resolute self-determination. But that road is not the only one or the best to use.

Self-determination is not a bad thing. We want to be in balance though. That means being willing to make key adjustments in our own attitude towards having to be rigidly self-sufficient by:

- Asking for help from experts

- Taking advice from people who have walked the same road

- Being willing to step outside of our comfort zone and by doing things differently

- Recognizing that we all have blind spots about ourselves, our beliefs and our behaviors.

- Giving up on pretending to look bulletproof. Sometimes we're more concerned with looking OK than being OK. Sometimes we decided in childhood that showing feelings of fear, sadness, despair or bewilderment is weak and should be squashed at all costs.

I was quite lucky I was so broken that my hard head finally became willing to take direction from others. I now know that I don't need to be roadkill again before I ask for help. The most amazing thing was that help and support appeared as if from nowhere once I became open to it.

It wasn't as if I didn't try. I did look for direction. I read every book I could lay my desperate hands on and went to five different psychologists – for years and years and years! But I still believed it was my job to fix myself. I was resolutely self-contained in front of them. One of them even called me a 'well-balanced individual'! Pish tosh I tell you! I was an unhappily married person who learned how to squash my own needs by focusing on all kinds of things outside myself, without any real tools for finding lasting inner happiness and serenity.

Being determined to solve your problems is not a bad thing. But we cannot see our own blind spots. And you cannot conjure coping tools from thin air! If your parents didn't possess these tools, because their parents didn't have them, then everyone just did the best they could. In turn we pass the lack of coping tools on to the next generation.

Sometimes we've saving people. A grandparent, a teacher, a co-worker… We're the lucky ones.

And sometimes we've to repeat the same mistakes over and over before we get ready to try something else and do the hard work of self-exploration. But it's so worth it and this book will help you do just that in a step-by-step way! I invite you to dive right in and take the self-empowerment steps that lead to fulfilling relationships and emotional freedom.

How To Use This Book

We're on an adventure here together to identify our pattern(s), to learn why we need these patterns, to identify and apply the tool sets that will help us make better choices and to navigate ourselves into better relationships.

I can guarantee you that some of the things you'll learn will surprise you. I am going to ask you to do counterintuitive things! It will be a journey, but if you stick with it and use this book in the way it's intended to be used – *as a workbook* – this will be a life changing experience. After all, your choices up to now have led you to pick up this book and therefore we're going to assume that you're aware

you need to change some habits and outlooks to get better results!

You can get your Workbook by downloading it on the last page of this book under *Resources.* Print it and use it well by writing as much as you need to in it.

This is an important moment, as this is where you take back your life and reroute it onto the road you want it to be on. I want you to make this momentous and worth celebrating by having a special file and maybe a good pen or beautiful colored markers. Start a dedicated 'me-time' ritual like getting your favorite beverage ready. Changing your life is about doing, not reading. Therefore I make suggestions and give assignments and practical exercises to do.

This is the first assignment! Make your Workbook, your time you spend on it and the place you work on it special! We've to learn to view ourselves as special and worth spending time, energy and money on if we want to make a positive change. So, start with a seemingly little thing.

I would love for you to share your special Workbook on our private Facebook page! Membership is free but curated to keep interaction, encouragement and inspiration to the highest standard.

Take your time, return to questions and be completely honest with yourself. If you keep at it with determination you can change your life. You have all the tools you need in here!

.

Part 1

IDENTIFYING PATTERNS

Sometimes our patterns are obvious. My father was an alcoholic and I knew from a young age that daughters of alcoholics are likely to marry an alcoholic themselves. My mother drilled into us the dangers of alcohol. She gave me articles to read that were clear about the likelihood of marrying an alcoholic. I was well informed. I knew I wouldn't be that stupid. I didn't want the life my mother had: the fights, the husband coming home drunk all hours, unreasonable about his cold supper. I knew that I didn't want a domineering, angry man. I wanted someone who saw me and loved me wholeheartedly.

We all do!

So, I fell for a funny, everyone's-friend-guy, who was head over heels in love with me. I was double-cream-cherry-chocolate-cheesecake to him. He was super helpful; he got along with everyone.

He didn't drink -

not in front of me anyhow.

He couldn't get enough of me. He helped my mother with all kinds of tasks a single mother needs help with. He phoned every day. He visited every weekend he could. He was helpful and kind to everybody he met. I laughed at his jokes. I admired his new car. I listened with rapt attention to his stories about his life growing up.

I married an alcoholic. He married an enabler.

But he didn't start out as an obvious alcoholic! Except that he had every single marker and trait right from the beginning.

Which is what this book is all about:

- About identifying the actual danger signs,

- Making more empowered choices, and

- Acquiring a tool set that will enable you to navigate through the inevitable drama until your discernment starts to improve.

Most of us have an idea of which patterns we don't want to repeat.

I definitely didn't set out to have a marriage that didn't work. For us the codependence worked for a long time. It was fifteen years of codependent messed-up bliss! I had such a deep belief that I couldn't fail in this marriage that I kept working at it even though I felt he was emotionally unavailable. I wanted to believe our relationship was my safe place to fall, so I had huge reactions, tears and begging when I found truths I didn't want to know. Having no idea which feelings were inside him was just an uncomfortable situation that I had to live with. The girls he flirted with didn't know that he was married but he explained it away as just 'his friendly nature'. The alcoholic friends he gravitated to were the ones with the problems, not him. The lies were accepted as plausible because I wanted to believe him. I didn't have sufficient resources within me to be without him. Our joint money disappearing couldn't be him. I eagerly hoped that this would be the last time every time I uncovered another stash of empty bottles.

That was when life was good, when he was head over heels in love with me, really repentant and loving and sweet every single day. All those unhappy things simply paled in comparison.

That was part of the fifteen years we were – mostly – happily married. Because we both didn't have enough self-insight and had a devastating lack of coping tools, we pushed every uncomfortable thing under the carpet. We lived and loved each other right over the lumpiness of that carpet.

So yes, we've a good idea which patterns we don't want to repeat:

We may be influenced by our own violent or hyper-critical father. Our primary father or mother figure may have been absent, physically or emotionally. Maybe he was angry, or weak and domineered by your mother. Maybe she favoured your brother and overlooked you completely. One or both may have been bad with money, dumping the family into financial disaster and hardship. We may have suffered through physical or emotional abuse. Addiction or unavailability due to mental challenges such as depression could have meant that you had to grow up way before you were supposed to. Your parents' relationship could have taught you that you were not safe, as at any moment it could all implode.

Our own position in the family influences the direction of our lives. Older children are often the hero who fixes everything and become the rescuer of the broken wing society. If there is a family member or a sibling who requires a lot of attention, you may become the invisible child who eases the family burden by not having any needs – the lost child! You may have decided your role is to detract attention from the drama by distracting everyone with your clowning around. Perhaps your only way to get attention was when you broke an arm. Possibly you were the scapegoat turned rebel. You may have given up trying, feeling as if you would never please one or both of your parents.

(You can read more on family patterns in *Perfect Daughters.*[1] You will find a list of Helpful Books under *Resources*.)

The families of our friends, our cousins and our grandparents also influence us. Sometimes we see relationships between a father and daughter that we crave, or mothers giving approval freely to their daughters. It may even have been *Little House on the Prairie* that influenced your idea of what you want!

In the end our subconscious distills a picture for us of what is safe. It instills craving in us of that which we wanted most: being important, being noticed, being seen, being accepted, and being safe.

These needs are the ones that will guide our decision-making. Our unconscious needs will likely be the thing that snares us into staying in a relationship way past the expiration date. It's our subconscious that is silently directing our actions and our often not-so-good choices. Our job is to identify this subconscious craving and neutralize it.

In the Workbook on page 4 is a great questionnaire that will give you much clarity on your habits, **so it's a great idea to complete it before you read the next section.** (You can get the Workbook by downloading it on the last page of this book under *Resources.*)

The Craving Inside Us Of Which We're Barely Aware

Most people go through life not knowing that we're being driven by a craving for love, acceptance, approval, support, belonging and connection – The Essential Six. How much or how little of these we received as children determines the extent of our craving later on.

(In your **Workbook** you'll find the first exercise to complete before you carry on.)

We're mostly completely unaware of the big craving inside ourselves, or we give it another name: "I have to finish a slab of chocolate when I start it" or "I cannot understand the reason I look for attention elsewhere when I have a good husband. Maybe he is not the one". "I want a baby" can mean "I desperately need to belong".

I ask "Where is the hole inside of you? Show me where in your body the hole is".

Nearly everyone can immediately point out exactly where in their body the hole is.

Go ahead. Try it.

Found it?

Oh heck...

We fill our lack of The Essential Six in the following ways:

- By finding people we get enmeshed with and by falling into codependent relationship patterns.

- Through over-working and excelling in what we do, we get external validation that makes us believe we finally have achieved self-worth. It's a wonderful driving force for achievement, but it doesn't get us the acceptance and connection we truly want, so we feel we've to work harder and achieve more; until we burn out.

- Having unsuitable friends that accept us. This may sometimes lead to becoming part of an alternative group culture in which we're not only accepted but celebrated for adapting an identity that differentiates us from the norm. We establish a counter-identity that feels more acceptable than our core self.

- Engaging in relationships in which we get admiration and adoration. This may be so self-affirming that we will endanger our core relationship and family values to get more of this 'fix'.

- Addiction [2] to any substance that dulls the pain and camouflages the lack of coping tools. Whether one uses alcohol, prescription medicine or a triple decker hamburger-with all-the-trimmings to deaden a-feeling-you-have-no-name-for and-no-help-for doesn't matter. What does matter is realizing it's all the same: a way to fill the hole.

- We substitute sex for authentic connection. It's easy to confuse the endorphin high and temporary connection we feel with a feeling of satisfaction. It could be through engaging in unsuitable relationship after relationship or full-out sexual addiction. In someone with a big emptiness inside them, the temporary illusion of connection feels so good that they will endanger themselves to have more and more of their fix. Even in a monogamous marriage we may be all about the sex if real connection is absent: We don't understand that what we crave inside is connection – to be seen and to be heard.

- Being so involved in other people's business that it becomes the focus of our existence. This could be your own children (excellent excuse, yes?) or anyone who dumps a problem into your inviting lap. You could find yourself in one of the 'helping professions' such as the entire medical spectrum from doctor to social worker or paramedic. Excellent excuse, once again! Caring for animals falls under these noble causes – there is nothing wrong with caring and helping, as long as you're not obsessed with it because subconsciously you're filling a hole. In these professions one can learn a balance in which one can choose to help because one can, not because one has to. One can still apply self-care and be in balance.

- Chasing something. Anything. New projects. More. It's never enough. A vague sense of discomfort and longing for something unknown steers our thinking and drives our actions.

- Distraction! From watching too much TV to over-committing yourself to sport or anything else, distraction can effectively deflect your attention away from your inner sense of unfulfillment. Yes, it works until the needs you're suppressing come out as volatile or reactive behavior, outright anger or passive aggressive behavior. You may feel it as 'depression'. Even worse, you can be misdiagnosed and labeled as being Bipolar or having Borderline Personality Disorder.

- Refusing to feel your feelings. The problem is that it will not work. You'll find an outlet in one of the behaviors above. You may get sick. The subconscious is keen to play along and distract us from emotional pain by giving us a believable alternative physical pain in our body to focus on instead. (Psychologically Induced Pain Syndrome PIPS[3])

Our relationship choices, patterns and woes are always about us. We like to think "If only he was like that" or "If he didn't do that" the relationship would be perfect – living happily ever after experiencing perfect happiness at last.

But that is fortunately not the way it works. I said *fortunately*!

The next section in the **Workbook** is titled *2. Patterns* Complete it before you continue reading.

Chapter 2

I Am Adored And Accepted

We're going to jump right in with THE BIG ONE!

Think back to the day you met.

The critical thing is to remember how you felt when you first connected. Take some time to write down the feelings you experienced.

'Special'. 'Could he really want *me*?' 'Warm', 'wanted', 'accepted', 'loved', 'amazing', 'I am someone', 'I belong'. Any or all of these feelings could be in the cocktail that makes up our love addiction.

Part of the head over heels tingly feeling is the knowledge of belonging. Belonging is the unrecognized drug that hooks us. There is not a better, warmer, cozier feeling in the world for us if we fit into this category. It's the drug that hooks us, and it has the ability to keep us hooked for much too long.

Being hooked on the feeling of belonging is such a primary human need that you cannot escape it. It keeps us locked in negative cycles, over and over and over.

A typical negative cycle may look like this:

Suzie has been married to her farmer husband for fourteen years. He's a good provider; he works diligently to provide everything their family of three young sons needs. But he's a stern, autocratic man who doesn't show his emotions. He's not approachable, nor does he invite opinions from others or welcomes family discussions. He believes that he's the only one who is right and being very successful in what he does reinforces that belief in him.

"The only way I ever get through to him is if I cry. I cry from sheer frustration and helplessness, and it gets him every time. Then he's comforting and apologetic and kind. He holds me and hugs me and brings me wild flowers from the fields because he knows that I love them. I get all hopeful and I feel inspired that we do have a chance at a proper relationship and I throw myself heart and soul into it again. But it doesn't last.

He promises to take my opinions into consideration but quickly it's back to his way and his opinions only.

"Those moments when it feels like he values me and hears me are the best times in our relationship. I recently started understanding that it's those short but amazingly good times that make me stick it out in a relationship in which I don't feel valued. I keep on wanting to believe it will now be different, and that we've finally had the conversation that will change how our relationship will be. I keep on believing because I want to believe."

Mary-Kate's story started differently:

"I never knew my father. He left us before my birth. I grew up with my mother and older brother in my grandparents' house. I think I did the predictable thing of looking for love in relationships. I got married to my first love when I was nineteen. We started dating when I was fourteen. Looking back, I realize that I kept pretending that he wasn't treating me badly.

"He was very jealous, but it felt great because I thought it meant that he loved me and that I was special to him. He had angry outbursts if he thought I was getting attention. I overlooked it as it made me feel attractive and desirable.

"After we got married it was better for a while. I was pregnant with our twins right away, and we were focused on bringing up our family. Having our own little family unit felt great, and for me it felt like I finally had the real family I had craved for so many years.

"His jealousy was always there but it only got out of hand when I started working, after the twins went to school. We needed the extra income, and I enjoyed being out among other grown-ups and finding out that I am good at my job. His cold silences and scathing, demeaning comments and angry outbursts would alternate with each other. I couldn't take it anymore and moved back in with my mother.

"Then he was all remorseful and promised to change and cried and said he couldn't live without us and he was so sweet and so convincing that we went back. Besides, I missed my own house and it sort of stinks for an intelligent, grown up woman to have to live with her mother. We did this six more times. I believed him every time because we felt so close and connected when he was sorry and crying and holding me and promising he would change.

"For some reason I believed I had to make this relationship work. Those times when he was remorseful felt so great and loving that it gave me courage to try again."

We easily remain stuck in a relationship that doesn't work, for whatever reason. If we leave without resolving our triggers and neutralizing our motivations, we end up back in the same relationship again. Sometimes even with the same man, sometimes with someone we thought was nothing like the first one!

> **Mary-Kate** finally left when he turned violent. She fell in love with a kind and gentle man who didn't bat an eyelid when someone paid her a compliment.
>
> "Ahhh, I thought, he is a keeper. What I didn't realize at the time was that his sense of self-esteem was exactly as non-existent as my first husband's. He couldn't make a single decision without my input. This time I wanted to do things differently. It was only during counseling that I recognized that I repeated my pattern of falling for men with low self-esteem who needed help. I am hooked the minute I feel connected to them and responsible for their happiness. I thought my pattern was 'jealous men'. Now I learned that it had more to do with my enormous need for belonging and finding self-worth. Through being there for the men who needed me to adjust in order to prop them up I found self-worth. I think my children gave me the courage to look for help, but now I realize that I also transferred my need to belong into my relationship with them."

Mary-Kate's need for belonging was so overwhelming that she didn't apply any discernment in her choice in men! She couldn't bear being on her own, and she jumped headlong into the next relationship in which she felt accepted and connected.

That sense of being accepted, feeling special and 'like we matter to someone' is enough to keep us hooked. Unfortunately, it will keep us hooked as long as we still have hope the relationship will improve. Our cells have memory of the first time we felt that feeling. It's the thing we've craved the most – unknowingly. Because it's such an undeniable part of human nature we stay way past the point where someone deserves our loyalty, because of that wonderful feeling!

We ignore the expiry date because we choose not to believe the obvious – that our own wants and needs are not met.

Transforming Activity (Workbook p. 6)

Reflect on this:

1. How you felt when you met that special person.

2. Is your loyalty something you easily give to people who are close to you or do they have to deserve it?

Chapter 3

I Am Needed

This one, being needed, is the second hook that locks us into trouble.

Self-Investigation (Workbook p. 6):

- How much of my time is spent solving other people's problems?

- Do I say "You must/You should/You have to" to my partner and other people?

- How much do I like it that people come to me with their problems?

- Am I willing to put aside my own needs because I feel their problems are more important?

- Do I feel 'selfish' if I express what I want?

- What are my partner's frailties that I recognized he needs me for?

- In which ways do I compensate for those challenges he experiences?

- What about myself do I change for my partner?

The thing to understand from the outset is that it takes two people to have a codependent relationship. It also takes two people to keep this dysfunction going. A dysfunctional relationship is never going to have one perfect partner and one scapegoat, although it's presented that way in many skewed relationships.

Every person can only work on their own part in the relationship, so we start with, "Which pattern am I contributing to?"

If you find yourself repeatedly being the one that helps others, the one who cannot (doesn't want to) say "No", the one people turn to for advice, the rescuer, the chairperson of the Broken Wings Society, you can be sure you're repeating that pattern in your relationship.

And if you do, you're doing it for a reason. You're doing it because you feel 'more' because of it. You're doing it because it makes you feel needed. You're doing it because it makes you feel important and indispensable. In short, you get self-esteem from it. And you'll not want to give it up until you learn to get self-esteem from a healthier source.

'I am needed' is the drug that keeps us enslaved to a bad relationship way past our understanding and our logical reasoning. It's the missing link that helps us understand how an accomplished, kind, capable woman can let herself be demeaned and undervalued.

This dangerous combination of feeling like we belong and feeling of value to someone else keeps us trapped. Problem is we're doing it to ourselves! This is good news, because it means we can change it!

The first thing to look at here is to notice how we're taking responsibility for other adults and putting our own needs on the back burner in order to be there for someone else.

We can call this our own kind nature, being a helpful person or being nice. Nothing wrong with that! But when we don't even have needs of our own or allow ourselves needs, we feel resentment because we don't get what we want deep down. We keep giving our needs up for others! Something is out of balance when our needs are hardly ever met, and we're being the 'nice girl' because of a strong inner need to belong, be useful, be important and be worthy.

Jennifer grew up in a home where her father was addicted to prescription medication. He was a well-respected, prominent businessman in their community, but a car accident left him in so much pain that he became addicted. The whole family pretended nothing abnormal was going on. From very young the children learned to cover up for him 'forgetting' to pick them up from school. They pretty soon worked out that it was better not to burden their frazzled, exhausted mother with their own needs. Instead Jennifer became her mother's main support and was valued for 'helping mommy'.

In adulthood Jennifer ended up in a marriage to an alcoholic. Once again, she was the mainstay, keeping the whole house together.

"It's just how I am. For as long as I remember I was always the one people could lean on. First, my mother, who used to tell me all her problems. Then my father, who didn't ask for anything or even communicated with me much. I knew I was to say he wasn't feeling well when he was like that again. I married a man who couldn't feel good about himself until he had had a drink, so I used to say mitigating things like, "The guys just need to unwind. They work so hard all week".

"It was so important to me to keep up the façade that everything was the way it was supposed to be. I never admitted to anyone how much energy it took to keep everything looking 'normal' to our friends and family. I was emotionally and physically exhausted but day by day I still managed to soldier on, and at night I took sleeping pills to wind down. I knew it was time to get help when I saw my daughter repeating my pattern in her marriage."

In relationships we automatically repeat this pattern of caring for others to the point that they don't need to take responsibility for their own problems. We find ourselves not having our wants and needs met and not even knowing that we can have wants and needs! What we do instead is being so busy filling up someone else's well that we don't notice how dry ours is running. We do know that we're desperately unhappy, lonely, unsupported and feeling empty!

We don't notice we're assuming responsibility for another adult's life. When we're in a relationship with such a person, we don't have a spouse or a mate, we've a project!

Dysfunctional and codependent relationships can work pretty well: Our partner needs propping up, rescuing, fluffing up, fussing over or practical things like sorting out financial messes. We keep giving to get the need for closeness and acceptance met (occasionally even). Or the other way around. I may need rescuing and he may need to feel like a hero. We may even be blissfully happy! When both partners keep getting and giving what the other dysfunctional partner wants, we can carry on like this indefinitely: 'Happily married ever after…'

Unfortunately, life doesn't work like this. Sooner or later someone grows up. Sooner or later someone gets fed up with not getting their needs met. One partner runs out of 'propping-up' steam. Someone stops needing to be propped up. Someone starts retaliating for not being propped up any more. Sooner or later passive aggressiveness, retaliation, withdrawal and punitive behavior turn the relationship into a battlefield of Hamster Wheel arguments.

My own marriage was a pretty convincing example of a dysfunctional marriage 'working' exceptionally well. Our friends used to say our marriage was an example of a perfect marriage.

I worked damn hard to make sure it looked that way!

Not on purpose though. I believed it was my job to make it work. For fifteen years I was determinedly happily married. For fifteen years we were besotted with each other. That was the part others saw. The hand-holding, the enmeshment. What they didn't see was that he headed straight for the drinks counter at any gathering, immediately downed at least three beers in a row, and I wouldn't see him again for the whole evening until we went home. And he pretended the beer I saw in his hand was the only one he'd had all night.

No one knew that he was drinking while I was at work, but never in front of me. No one knew of all the lies and denials or about all the empty bottles I found hidden away. I thought I was going crazy. He said he loved me, and would absolutely not drink because he knew how hard it was for me growing up with an alcoholic father. He acted as if I was unreasonable for not believing him about his 'one beer'. He was completely shocked to think I could suspect him of drinking during the day when I wasn't home. He only had a coke when he was visiting friends. How could I even think of accusing him of being drunk! It's only eleven in the morning after all!

But he loved me, and adored me, and accepted me, and thought I was wonderful. I needed that more than food or water. It was what I craved more than anything my whole life. I could put my unhappiness regarding his lies to one side, as long as he loved me unconditionally. It was never a conscious decision, but somewhere inside me I knew I could take anything as long as he adored me.

Stepping in to prop up his precariously low self-esteem was a conscious decision though. I was only sixteen years old when we met, but within the first week I saw he was exaggerating and embellishing his stories. Even at that age I knew it meant he had low self-esteem. I consciously decided I would laugh at his jokes, give him non-stop compliments and fluff him up until he felt better about himself. That didn't work, by the way! But it did serve to solidify our enmeshment. Because now he was my project who needed me. And I was only sixteen.

What if my partner truly does need help?

Being a kind and helpful human being is an admirable thing. No one wishes you to be different.

It's only a problem:

- When you're not in balance because you don't put yourself in the queue and you don't have "No" in your vocabulary.

- If you're disempowering someone by preventing his negative consequences. Learning that actions have repercussions is part of being a responsible adult. Allowing someone to be their own adult and to grow in spite of your own fears is admirable and the kindest thing you can do.

- If you assume that your partner is not responsible for his own problems It's fully reasonable to expect of another adult to find their own help for problem behavior. You don't need to make allowances for unacceptable behavior because you're sorry for him or understanding of the circumstances. You can still be empathetic and encouraging though.

A strong need for belonging and an equally strong need to feel important because of being needed are not a lasting foundation for a happy relationship. It's the chains that keep us locked into unhappiness.

Self-Investigation (Workbook p. 8)

When I know my hidden needs and triggers, I can change them by putting other values in their place.

1. Does it make me feel safe to be indispensable?

2. Do I feel good when I rescue people?

3. Do I feel obliged to say "Yes"?

4. Am I so busy in other people's lives because then I don't have to look into my own dramas?

5. Do I choose to be involved in other people's dramas because I don't have any tools with which to solve my own issues?

6. Do I over-concern myself with the other person's reasons for dysfunction as that deflects attention from my own responsibility?

7. Do I feel great if I can be of value? Does it feel good to be needed?

The more questions you answer 'yes' to, the lower your self-esteem score is. Knowing that you're challenged in the self-esteem department and understanding why you are, empowers you to make meaningful changes.

Transforming activity:

This is your week for saying "No!" You can make it easier on yourself by warning people around you that you're going to say "No", but that you still love them; you're only taking better care of yourself. See how many 'no's' you can tally up in a week! Be kind, not apologetic. Be firm, not stand-offish or rejecting.

I was in awe of an employee who told me, "No, I cannot" when I asked her to work an extra day. No excuses, no tone. Way to go!

Chapter 4

Learned Helplessness – Needing A Caretaker

Clarifying Questions (Workbook p. 9):

- Do I head straight from one relationship to the next?

- Do I believe deep down that I need someone to take care of me?

- Am I aware that I have excellent qualities but only feel complete with a man around me?

- What are my views on women's and men's roles in relationships?

- What did my mother teach me about being self-sufficient? Did she think it was a great thing or did she warn me that it may frighten men away?

- And my father? Did he trust my judgment and praise my abilities? Did he have confidence in me?

Jilly has been married three times. She is a smart, capable and drop-dead-gorgeous thirty-six-year old. Every business venture she starts turns into gold.

Yet she cannot bear to be without a man to take care of her. After her last marriage her twin daughters begged her to stay single for a while, but the first man she met online was 'the one'. She moved in within three weeks of meeting him.

I asked her to explain why she doesn't give herself time to be on her own.

"Growing up my mother didn't approve of anything I did. She double-checked everything and never praised me for using my own initiative. I remember when I started taking an interest in cooking. One holiday she wanted me to roast a beef sirloin the way she showed me. I found a recipe for making a casserole and I spent the whole day cubing the meat and cutting the vegetables and making stock. I was so proud of myself! My mother took one look at it when she arrived home, pulled her face in disgust and said she wasn't hungry.

"The rest of us ate in deadly silence. They finished it all! It was actually delicious.

"But mine tasted like cardboard.

"I guess it was this kind of thing that still makes me feel like someone should supervise me.

"My father was a whole different story. He was quiet and gentle, but I cannot even remember how many times he told me to find a good fellow who can take care of me. It was as if at no time it even entered his mind that I can take care of me. Even now, when I know that I am capable and clever and good with money, some part of me still doesn't believe it."

Part of being an adult is understanding that we're responsible for our own happiness, our own way in life and our own self-esteem. When we find ourselves incapable of embracing our own strengths and capabilities, it's time to decide if this is a rational observation, or unfounded in truth. Our job is to investigate through which eyes we're judging ourselves. Our job is to find out whose opinions (founded in their own hurts) have we made our own.

If it's a belief unsupported with facts and evidence, then it's time to find out why we don't believe in our own power as an adult.

Nancy had an undiagnosed learning problem. "Ever since I went to school I believed I wasn't as acceptable as the others. I was astonished when Peter asked me out on a date. This guy was clever – why would he want to be with me? Needless to say that I exhausted myself trying to look perfect and not slip up and let anyone see I didn't fit in. This went on with every guy I dated, until I met Jason.

"I fell pregnant and we got married, but I still didn't feel I could make decisions without him. Luckily his work took him away for long periods, and I had to figure out most of the motherhood journey on my own. And I was great at it.

"It took me long to recognize that I am actually not stupid. My son needed special glasses for dyslexia, and that opened the whole wide world for me! After I got my own pair of special glasses I enrolled for a degree and did exceptionally well. But I still double-checked all my decisions with Jason. I didn't want to make a mistake and feel stupid! It wasn't that I was stupid, it was that I was so scared of looking stupid that I double- and triple-checked everything with Jason.

"Now I finally am learning to trust my own input and to like myself. I recently noticed that I was putting a huge burden on Jason by not contributing my views and input, as two heads are better than one. He finally shared with me how exhausting it was for him to shoulder so much on his own because I refused to make decisions."

Sometimes we get lucky and we manage to prove ourselves dead wrong!

(Find your Transforming Activity in the **Workbook p. 10**)

Chapter 5

I Am So Good At Being The Rescuer

Traditionally the oldest child is often the hero in the family. This is even more true if we had to overcome trauma growing up and found ourselves in the caretaker-rescuer-savior-role. This is because we had to learn how to be a little adult long before we should have had those responsibilities. (Find your own dominant familial roles by investigating the roles on **page 10 in the Workbook.)**

This can become so entrenched in our behavior that we make a lifelong habit of setting ourselves up in that position. We get value from being this savior person and accept it as part of our personality.

Popular movies like *Pretty Woman* illustrate this for us, but what we don't understand is how often this plays out in everyday life.

We more often see this where single women, with or without children, are being rescued and taken care of by a financially stable man. This is the nature of our patriarchal society, with men being taught from a young age to be providers and feeling worthy because of that role.

And yes, there have been and always will be cases where a woman is financially stable and a good provider and she treasures her ability to provide for a man. She may even prefer that kind of relationship, as this way she doesn't feel beholden to anyone and has a little bit of security in knowing she is needed. No one likes being abandoned, and being the provider buys a measure of protection against it. Being indispensable can be used as a weapon. It can be purposefully created by a woman unsure of her ability to keep a man based purely on her own belief of not being acceptable and wanted for herself.

But this is not as simple as just finances. Women can apply the same rescuing/fixing/saving tactics as Richard Gere's character in the movie and feel morally and socially superior. Women also claim for themselves the right to 'mold' someone else into their vision of what is good and appropriate for another.

- You perhaps feel morally superior and try to shame and guilt him into attending church.

- You may have an excellent education, and in your eyes his simple ways need improving.

- You may deplore his lack of dress sense and his lack of your kind of style, and make sure you instruct him in acceptable ways – according to your likes and dislikes.

- You may look down on his family and feel quite superior to them. After all, your family is the well-known Joneses, and you seldom miss an opportunity to let him know in which ways his family is inferior to yours.

But maybe you're just a really nice kind of person; nothing of this superiority nonsense – it was obvious how much he needs you to sort out his life. You'll not dream of disparaging his parents, or his job or his friends.

You'll rescue him from his bad financial managing, from his user friends, and his sponging sister. Because you're a nice, caring, capable person. You'll gladly buy him new clothes when he needs them because he sucks at it, shame. You'll decide what everyone is getting for Christmas, because shame, he is so bad at it. You'll do his taxes, because shame, he is so forgetful.

You'll take over his life with the best intentions and you'll feel good because you know it's your responsibility to help him straighten out his life. He may even feel grateful and relieved.

Until he starts resenting you because he does not feel like an adult.

Linn did everything for her husband. She laid his clothes out in the morning, ran his errands and managed the household like Superwoman. This worked well for a long time, but gradually Linn started picking up little barbs from Henry. At first, she barely noticed it. I mean, she is a busy woman! It was just one more thing to manage.

Then she had to notice it. The barbs turned into coldness, disdain, disparagement and disconnection. "I felt that a stranger moved into my house and bed. It was the age-old story of the wife being the last to notice. How humiliatingly predictable! He worked longer hours, was permanently tired, and wasn't interested in sex anymore. One New Year's Eve my senses suddenly lit up when I intercepted the look that passed between him and my closest friend. It was all there on his cell phone and his emails. Even the 'likes' on his Facebook page…

"He simply said she made him feel like a man. I felt like I was hit by a wet fish. This is the same man who loved it when I did his shopping and his taxes! It took me years to get over him and start trusting someone again. I never ever wanted to expose myself to that kind of rejection again. It hurt too much to be thrown away like that. I was physically sick to my stomach and locked in a dark place for a long time. Even someone mentioning her name in passing caused me to have a panic attack.

"I finally was persuaded to go on a blind date with a man who lost his wife to cancer after thirty years of being happily married. That was the deciding factor. He stood by her through her illness and was faithful for thirty years. This was a safe man! I immediately realized the poor man couldn't cook an egg! I helped him restock his pantry and throw out the clothes that fell into disrepair during his wife's illness. Our relationship is becoming quite close, but I do notice worrying signs that he is distant sometimes.

"I was quite lucky that my doctor suggested counseling when the panic attacks returned. That was when I learned about my true pattern. It wasn't falling for unfaithful men. It was falling for helpless men. My panic attacks were over loss of connection when the men in my life withdrew from my way of taking over!

"That was a very painful moment.

"I loved being the savior."

Even though Linn was mortified when she recognized her true pattern, that was the moment when she could take her power back and change her life.

Our patterns are never based on the other person, the 'guilty' party, the 'perpetrator'.

Our patterns are consistently stemming from ourselves. There is a reason we stay in relationships that have stopped working or are downright toxic to us. There is a reason we get into relationships in the first place – even when we know something is not right and we choose to ignore the warning bells!

The reason for this is not our kind heart, our caring nature or our conscience that tells us to go through with it. It's the need inside of us that is being met, that nudges us along, headlong into disaster.

My own needs kept me trapped when my 'happily-dysfunctional' marriage turned into years of desperate unhappiness, loneliness, confusion about where our connection went and desperation to find a way to fix it.

Somewhere after his fortieth birthday it started. All of a sudden, he developed depression. He stopped smoking. When his father passed away his world moved on its axis. And then there's this thing they don't tell us: men over forty often get depressed as their hormone levels start to go down. But that was only the beginning...

The attentive, loving, funny, kind guy I was married to disappeared.

In his place was someone who couldn't find a single good thing about life. He was increasingly grumpy with huge mood swings. He was impulsive and accident prone, but now on a much bigger scale.

When he was finally diagnosed with ADD (Attention Deficit Disorder) everything fell in place. The need for high action adventure, his disorganization, the addictive personality, being easily triggered into hyper-activity as well as the low energy bouts - these were just some of the inexplicable things I lived with for so long. I didn't feel like I was going crazy anymore; I finally had something that made sense of the chaos that was our life. When he stopped smoking the symptoms suddenly amplified, as he was effectively self-medicating with smoking!

For me it was a relief. For him it was a shame-filled sentence. He had wanted to be like everyone else since he could remember. So, it took a long time before he accepted that he has ADD, embraced it, and learned coping tools. But that was only one side of the coin.

We didn't know anything about Dry Drunk Syndrome. When you experience what Dry Drunk Syndrome does is when you know what an emotional desert feels like.

When you're an alcoholic, there is a set of typical behaviors based on your lack of emotional coping skills and missing problem-solving tools. When you get sober on your own without professional help, you can still have those behaviors. You're grandiose, emotionally absent, irritable, unpredictable and resentful. Yes, and then there is the ADD thing… Combine the two and suddenly you find yourself alone. Your husband is gone. The attentive guy who without fail held your hand and gave you compliments and who was big on physical touch left. In his place is someone who is critical, rejecting, absent, passive aggressive, irrational, and illogical. And he totally rejects you. Overnight.

You keep trying because you once were loved. For twelve years you live in a confusing emotional drought where you don't even know yourself anymore. Where did the together, happy, positive, proactive person who used to live in your body go? Who is this person who gave up, who is unhappy every single day and who has nothing left to give anyone else?

Until you know that you cannot do this for one more day.

My own needs kept me trapped. I felt I had to fix the relationship at all costs. I didn't understand that I had to fix 'me'.

Once we develop the ability to decipher the need inside that causes this strong invisible push or pull inside us, we're free to make better choices.

Transforming Activity:

Do you find yourself being the rescuer or caretaker of another adult/s? Spend some time on the really important questions on **page 13 in the Workbook.**

It's a heavy load and a big responsibility.

I experienced the load we take onto ourselves by being everything for everyone. I had been burdening myself for the longest time with being other people's caretakers and preventer-of-disasters and improver-of-other-people. It's a heavy burden and, in the end, we're baffled and lonely and depleted and left without the support and connection we so desire.

There is a better way, and we will investigate the tools soon.

More identifying of patterns first!

Chapter 6

Runaway – Now You See Me, Now You Don't!

Let's answer these questions first:

- Do you fall for unsuitable, unavailable partners? These could be married men or emotionally distant partners. You could also prefer relationships with people who live or work far away.

- Do you do things to sabotage the relationship? Do you find fault or withdraw when someone gets close? Do you engage in affairs or flirting as a means of getting kicked out of a relationship?

- Are your partner/s of choice too young to be considered seriously, or dangerous for some reason?

- Would this be someone your parents would heartily disapprove of?

- Do you throw yourself 590% into that thing you do? Work or running or the hobby that is taking over your life. Are you so involved in other people's lives that you cannot look at your own? Are you a workaholic?

- And then there is addiction. Are you self-medicating with any kind of substance that makes things easier to handle? Does it make you feel more 'in' and acceptable? Is it giving you that rush you so desperately need to feel OK? Chocolate, anyone? What are you filling that hole inside you with?

We're often not aware that what we're doing is running! Dating is not running, is it?

But it could well be! If we look at our habits and every time we come up against the same thing – unsuitable – we've to ask ourselves this:

Is this fear of intimacy?

or

My inner rebel is alive and kicking,

thank you very much!

Sandy was preached into submission for as long as she could remember. Her overly religious dad did everything but a virginity test when she started dating. If you could call it dating! In fact, it was awkwardly holding hands with boys whose parents were in the same church. They got her father's approval.

"I was always the good girl. My friends were getting up to all sorts of fun, but mostly I wasn't permitted to go with them, or I had to be back before dark, if I was allowed to go at all. There was no reason for his scrutiny. I wanted to be good! But no matter what I did, my dad never believed me. I had no way of being good enough for him.

"I clearly remember the day I knew that I wouldn't ever be able to get his trust. I came home twenty minutes late from choir practice because I helped an old lady with her parcels. Earlier I'd said no to this gorgeous boy who wanted me to go on a picnic with him and his parents. I knew my dad wouldn't let me go. They were not in our church. All my friends were excited about a dance at the school. I said I had to study.

"And he called me a lying slut because he drove past as I said no to this boy.

"That is the day I gave up on him.

"That is the day I turned into a rebel."

Sandy's journey started with smoking and making friends with girls she knew her dad would disapprove of. She sneaked out to meet dangerous boys; the ones she knew her dad would outright condemn. Her path led her to promiscuity but miraculously she managed to get herself to adulthood relatively unharmed.

But her inner rebel directed every relationship she managed to get herself into.

Dad won't like him. Tick!

Her responsible inner girl took over as she was set to marry husband number four, because by now she had a gorgeous four-year-old. And finally, she understood that being a rebel wasn't working for her.

"Through some miracle I registered that green hair and tattoos and dangerous men were not going to work if I wanted to give my boy a better life. I had to get counseling to reconnect to who I started out as before hurt turned me into a rebel. I learned it was time I made decisions that were good for me, not to spite my dad. I am now learning I can combine my individuality and love of adventure with responsibility to myself and my kid. Treating myself with loving compassion and learning that I am an adult who has the right to my own choices and my own consequences took the fight right out of me."

On the complete opposite side of the spectrum are those of us who've been hurt to the core, and who have lost our ability to trust and open up.

This is often, but not always, true for victims of abuse: sexual or physical or verbal. On the one hand there is a desperate need to feel belonging and closeness and on the other well-grounded fear and mistrust of others.

(Sexual abuse is a complicated issue and needs an in-depth focus as so many factors influence the outcome in your life: From who the abuser was, to your mother's reaction, to how often and how long, and from what age it started and if you fought back or said, "Stop, no more". Professional assistance is recommended to work through the fallout. It would be disrespectful for me to try and handle it in a mere paragraph, but we will take it into consideration as respectfully as possible.)

What we do know is that our fear is usually not unknown to us. It's often a conscious decision not to expose ourselves to hurt again.

We know if it's because we've been physically hurt or stripped of our self-worth through relentless disparaging of our core selves. We know when we've been rejected and left for another. We know when we've been held captive in a demeaning relationship by financial need. We know when we've been sexually disrespected. We know what it feels like if alcohol or another addiction is more important than us.

Fear of abandonment and fear of being hurt again are different from other patterns, because we consciously choose to hold on to our hurt like a shield. Sometimes we prefer not to get involved at all, but often our human need to belong wins out. Then we tend to choose someone non-threatening according to our own paradigm.

We may do that in relationship after relationship. We may even do this in the hurtful relationship we cannot leave for some reason relating to our own unconscious needs.

It looked like this for me:

I had been rejected so many times by my husband who used to adore me that I eventually gave up. I tried everything I knew for twelve years, but I eventually ran out of options. I went into helpless-and-hopeless for two years of my life. I decided I would learn not to care about him. I decided I would learn to not love him. As a twelve-year-old I managed to stop caring about my parents who were not there for me. I could do it again. I became unavailable emotionally. I stopped trying. I decided that I wouldn't expose myself to being rejected even one more time. I wouldn't be hurt that way again.

That was my own story. Sadly, it's true for anyone who chooses to stay in a relationship in which they were severely hurt and traumatized. It's hard work to learn how to touch the stove plate again; to learn how to trust and try again.

The fear of the hot stove plate is your transference of your fears from a previous relationship or hurts from your childhood into a new relationship. That would be classified under 'baggage'!

Your fears could be caused by affairs, neglect, abusive language, rejection of your core being, dominance, someone else preferred over you, loss of self or losing your belief system that your home and relationship are safe havens in the world. Whatever caused you to be so traumatized can influence how you are in future relationships.

You can jump into another relationship headlong to mask feeling abandoned, like the person who goes out to get another puppy when hers is run over. Or you can be overly cautious about allowing yourself to feel any real emotion.

You can also choose unsuitable partners as a protective measure.

Sometimes unsuitable partners have less to do with a remembered hurt, but more to do with a deep core belief that we ourselves are basically unwanted, unlovable and unacceptable human beings. If we choose unsuitable partners, we can move on before our basic unacceptability is found out! We don't have to give so deeply of ourselves. We don't even have to consider vulnerability.

Melany kept choosing partners she wasn't that into. "I knew that if I didn't like them that much, it would be easier when they eventually found out that they didn't want me after all. I didn't understand my deep-seated belief that I am an unacceptable person kept me from committing myself deeply. It was easier than being abandoned by someone I deeply cared about."

Nadine kept falling for married men. "They couldn't reject me because they were not available. I firmly believed I wouldn't survive another rejection after my failed marriage."

Denise is only interested in long-distance romances. "I had an overwhelming commitment fear. I was so smothered by my mother and father while growing up that I vowed on no account to let it happen again. Luckily, I learned that through firm boundaries and self respect I can now be in a loving, committed relationship."

Patti's husband left her for his much younger mistress. Her self-confidence was rock bottom. When a much younger man went gaga over her, she started a pattern of only getting involved with younger men. "I felt so bad about myself that Shaun's attention was heaven sent." She is now repairing her self-esteem and a man's integrity, sense of humor and how he treats her are her most important guide.

None of our triggers are simple or in isolation. They are hidden from us and are influenced by:

- Our life circumstances

- Our conditioning during childhood

- Our learned fears

- Our enabling support groups (or lack of support), and

- Our limiting beliefs.

We may have a bit of this trigger, and a lot of the other. Or some of the one pattern, but most of another pattern. Or bits of all of them!

The important thing is to identify what is relevant and take action!

Transforming Activity (Workbook p. 14):

Running away, being a rebel and withdrawing our emotions are self-protective measures.

1. Which feelings do you rather squish than experience?

2. Who makes you feel powerless?

3. What do you do when you feel judged or rejected?

4. Which activity makes you feel better about yourself?

Now rewrite your life:

1. How can I express that feeling without blaming, demoralizing or minimizing myself?

2. How can I step into my power as an adult? What needs to happen?

3. Which empowering words can I calmly speak when I feel judged or rejected? How can I say that I feel hurt without playing the victim role?

4. Which activity is healthier and more empowering than the way in which you currently run away?

Chapter 7

Can It Be That You Are In An Abusive Relationship?

Abuse comes in many forms. Our childhood scars as a result of a traumatic upbringing take dedication and often need skilled professional help to overcome. Additionally, being treated in an abusive way in our adult relationships is soul destroying and demoralizing to the point that we've to claw our way back day by day to a semblance of our authentic self.

What abusive relationships have in common is that we lose who we are. We lose our individuality, our sense of a separate self. We lose our ability to see the bigger picture as we become part of someone else's puppet show. We end up powerless as we forget that we're adults with choices.

There are endless 'have to's and 'ought to's and 'shoulds' and 'should nots' in abusive relationships. Someone is repeatedly imposing their views and their wants on another human being. In the process that person gives up what they value and ends up being a shell of themselves.

In your **Workbook on page 16** you'll find a questionnaire about the signs of abuse you may be experiencing.

Some of it may surprise you, as we tend to think of abuse as being violent, angry, loud and overbearing. It could be and often is, as we're frequently easily manipulated and intimidated by someone's anger.

Yes, you may be bullied into submission by someone ignoring your turn to speak or talking louder.

You may be called names and belittled.

You may be emotionally manipulated through someone using guilt and blame on you.

However, someone withholding their affection to get you to comply is as abusive as a slap and even more effective!

Being in an abusive situation is not about the perpetrator. It's about ourselves. If we reflect back to who we were before we walked into an abusive relationship, are we not going to see someone with hope and spunk and dreams for herself? I am talking about relationships in which you committed freely, moved in quite happily, and stayed and stayed. I am not talking about someone being captured and held bound and gagged. I am talking about an adult woman who has given up her right to self-determination. Abuse is about the perpetrator. Remaining in an abusive relationship is about ourselves.

I often find that those being abused have stopped noticing the inappropriateness of the tactics employed against them. I often have a client telling me their life story and it will sound something like this:

"I don't get asked for my opinion. The girls and Johnnie just decide where we're going on holiday. But it's OK because I want them to be happy."

How is it OK?

"Every night of the week there is some sort of gathering in the pub after work, and he comes home drunk every time. He says the job is stressful and they are just letting off steam."

How is it OK?

"I just put up with it because I don't want to be the nagging party pooper wife."

How is it OK?

"We've these sessions where we don't speak to each other, because I didn't agree with him."

How is it OK?

"He has long text messages with this woman friend of his. I don't want to look like a jealous wife, so I say nothing, even though she gets more attention than I do. She is married too, he says, therefore it's OK."

How is it OK?

"He never ever has time to do any of the things I ask him to do around our home, but every weekend he is somewhere helping one of his friends."

How is it OK?

"He spends thousands on himself. I have not bought myself anything new in ages because there is no money for that."

How is it OK?

"When we were dating you kissed that fellow, so I will never trust you again."

How is that OK?

We're either so trained in childhood into ignoring pink elephants in the room, or we're so scared of losing someone's affection, or we've given up so much of ourselves in the relationship that we stop seeing the inappropriateness of the other person's behavior. We can clearly see when a friend is disrespected or not appreciated. In turn, we sit in the steadily heating water not noticing a thing. Until we get burned badly.

Transforming Activity (Workbook p. 18):

1. Why did I give up my power as an individual?

2. How do I get it back?

3. And how do I not ever make the same mistake again?

Why Do We Have These Patterns?

The negative mental material you're working with could be from adulthood, including current experiences. But it's often important to address explicit and implicit memories from your childhood, since these are usually the taproots of the things that keep upsetting you.

– Rick Hanson

We're a curious mixture of DNA, unconscious behaviors learned in childhood, remembered lessons, conscious decisions, influence from our surroundings and influence from the people in our life.

We will look at all of these through questionnaires that will help us uncover our unconscious learning. The best way to answer these questions is by going through them slowly and coming back to them the next day. Some of us have poor childhood memories because of traumatic suppression. If that is you it helps to have an (out-loud) conversation with your unconscious mind before you go to bed:

> *"Dear Unconscious Mind,*
> *Thank you for protecting me from hard things when I needed it*
> *but I don't need you to protect me anymore. I'm now an adult*
> *with choices and support, and you can stop protecting me."*

A word of caution though – depending on the level of trauma you experienced you may need professional support during this phase. You can experience feeling like scrambled eggs. You can be very emotional for a while as you process the previously suppressed emotions that are suddenly available to you. There is nothing wrong with that. Talk therapy during this time will be helpful as it will help you to sort through your jumbled emotional reactions and transform past events into manageable experiences.

Writing letters never-to-be-posted is another way of processing pent-up emotions and re-ordering them.

It's never about blame, though! This exercise is about understanding. Once we understand our learned behaviors, triggers and patterns we can use our positive lessons to our advantage. We can choose what we want to do with the lessons that don't serve us well: we can discard limiting beliefs, we can find gratitude for our lessons, we can learn coping tools where we lack them, and we can change behaviors that harm us.

The third powerful tool of healing is being part of a community going through the same thing. The Facebook Support Group is there for you and I invite you now to share what came up for you. It's a safe, anonymous place to unburden and get support from others who understand what you're working through. (The Facebook link is under *Resources* in the back of the book. Feel free to ask questions as you read. I am happy to answer them.)

Awareness is key

Awareness is being present in your own life

- It's being aware of our motivators.
- It's neutralizing compulsive behaviors.
- It's being aware of what is holding us back.
- It takes away the power of triggers over us.
- It takes away distortions in our views of ourselves and others.
- It gives us the power to choose our responses instead of being a bundle of reactions.
- It decreases rigidity in attitude and improves decision-making skills and conflict resolution skills.

Awareness gives us the ability to be fully present in our life in the present moment.

To increase our awareness, we take the time to read about other people's experiences, ask ourselves hard questions and reflect carefully on which triggers are applicable in our own relationships.

When an adult engages in the clinical work of examining their use of the emotional and mental information from childhood, they bring into their control the choices associated with adult relationships and functioning. As their awareness grows, they gradually change the behaviors that don't support the healthy adult life they envision for themselves as members of their community, family and primary partnerships. Leaving the prisons of their past, they are freed into a world of possibilities where they can more fully and consciously enjoy their lives.

– Margaret Meinecke, LCSW, CAC III[4]

Chapter 8

Mother's Delight?

'cause I'm your mother," said the Narcissist
If it hadn't been for you. I
would have had everything. you
ruined my life. I

wish you'd never been born.
I lost my teeth because of you. giving birth
to you caused my hair to fall out. don't think
that you're better than me. I

don't know where you came from.
you don't get to be upset. you're
lucky I kept you. no one
wants to look at your face. you'll never

be smarter than me.
I need to get my life together. I
can't help you. paying
your rent before helping me. you
ain't never been shit.

– Vivian Blac[5]

We start with one of our biggest unconscious triggers:

How did you please your mother?

It would be most helpful to complete your questionnaire on **page 19 in the Workbook** before you read further.

Our primary caregivers have the greatest lifelong influence on us, until we become aware of our unconscious driving forces. Then we can change them into a guide that is more compatible with where we want to be in life.

When we look at our current relationships patterns we start by thoroughly and carefully examining the influence of the person we've the strongest biological bond with — mother dearest.

My mother said things like "Being an alcoholic is hereditary"; "You'll never have friends"; "Your children will be as difficult as you"; "You're just like your father."

She didn't outright condemn men, but I observed as the married men circled our house, calling "I know you're lonely" at the windows. My brother and I were hiding under the dining room table with her, as quiet as mice – it was then that I knew men are not to be trusted.

She didn't once attend my prize-givings or sports events. But she very much liked me to make her tea. So I ended up having a restaurant for fifteen years, which I couldn't give up even when my health suffered. Until I realized why! I'd been doing the one thing my mother approved of – making tea or food. Unknowingly I toiled all those years trying to fill that approval-void my upbringing left in me. I found a vocation in the only thing my mother appreciated me for! To put this in perspective: I have a degree and had a successful career with great prospects. Yet I chose to work sixteen hours a day in a restaurant, harming my own health with the long hours I chose myself. It puts a whole different perspective on the power of our hidden childhood cravings, does it not? Now that I've successfully healed this wound by loving myself, you can hardly convince me to throw a dinner party. But for years I had invisible prison bars around me.

Sometimes it's not what they say, but what they do or don't do.

Lynette's mother was in one abusive relationship after the other. She didn't know how to say "No". The only times she ever left was when the children were in danger.

"I was twelve years old when I decided that I would never let a man treat me like that. I despised my mother for taking that abuse and was seething for a long time because she didn't take better care of us. I want to be with a good, kind, strong man, but I think I choose a weak man time after time because I fear being dominated so much. Eventually I find I have no respect for him and I start despising him, and I get quite mean. It's a mess."

Lisa's story sounds different: "My mother domineered my father. I have absolutely no respect for him. In fact, she controlled all of us. I have no idea who I am, as she told me my entire life what to do, what not to do, what to wear, who to be friends with... I thought we were close, but in reality, I was just completely controlled. Like my father. Now I find I cannot forgive myself for being as weak as my father.

"I gave up on relationship after relationship as the men I was dating all fell short of her expectations. I broke my own heart over and over to please her. No more! I am now in a relationship with a great man. With help from my counselor I am determined to carve out my own life and trust my own choices, even though once again she disapproved of my partner."

Some of us are motivated by positive reinforcement: "You're such a good girl" and "You're mommy's little helper."

"Nice girls don't get angry." Nice girls don't..." The list is endless! The ultimate goal becomes being a nice girl according to someone else's standards.

Some of us heard things like "Suzy is the pretty one and Petra is the clever one." And we believed the labels and live up to them.

Then there is the absent mother. This could be because she is so overwhelmed by being the glue that keeps the family together that she barely has energy left for the children. Instead she starts needing them to support her. Sometimes there are addiction or mental health issues.

Janet tells us of her experience: "My mother never recovered from my little brother dying of meningitis when he was four years old. We learned to tippy toe around her. She was in her darkened room a lot. When she was around she by no means really connected with us. It wasn't until our teenage years before we understood she was addicted to Valium – which the doctor prescribed! She did get help eventually and got better when my father left, but we're all seriously messed up today. My brother's marriage is falling apart, and my sister is a hardcore rebel who constantly needs us to bail her out of her messes. I am such a people pleaser that I hate myself."

Tara shares her story: Her mother worked long hours and she willingly took care of the two younger children because that got her approval from her mother. Her older sister was lying and stealing but could do anything wrong in her mother's eyes. The double standards were too much for her to watch. At sixteen she took a part-time job.

"I knew I had to get out of the house and worked from that time to have money of my own and buy a motorbike as my ticket to freedom. Fiona was my mother's favorite. Even though she had an explosive temper and I had to protect the two younger ones, she was never reprimanded. She became a binge drinker by 16 years old, which I am certain both parents knew about and thought was funny. I lived my entire life trying to get the same approval as Fiona. I was forty-one years old before I understood what I was looking for."

Tara had to learn to become less affected by her mother's opinion and trust her own judgment more. Wanting our mother's approval is a strong underlying driving force, as it's such a primal need. If we never had it, it's a contributing factor to the hole inside us. If we did have it, we recreate that feeling by repeating the actions that got us the original approval. Tara's mother approved of her taking care of the younger kids. Tara is still in a care profession today.

(Note: If we've been conditioned to be rescuers, enablers and dependent on others' approval, we're likely to end up in one of the 'care professions': nursing, doctors, paramedics, the counseling professions, welfare workers or in the police or fire brigade.)

Mother and daughter patterns

We fall into one of a few categories:

- The absent mother. Whether she died, left you with someone else or wasn't emotionally present for you, this is the ultimate rejection and abandonment. Perhaps she didn't bond with you. It could be she had negative associations with your conception and birth.

- Completely emotionally distanced from your mother, trying to avoid contact as much as possible. She may make overtures, but you have lost your belief in it being any good for you. On the face of it you seem polite and behave daughter-like, but you're not available to be hurt.

- Appearing to be compliant, but secretly resenting all the guilting and victimhood she manipulates you with. It slowly builds up and may result in you letting off steam through explosive outbursts.

- You feel like a respected adult and genuinely love spending time with your mother. In adulthood you have found a new mutually supportive relationship where both value the other's contribution.

- You share everything with your mother and don't feel whole without continuous contact or her input. You have a very close connection, but you're aware that others question your relationship.

- You feel utterly dependent on her approval yet bitterly resent her. You're so enmeshed that you find yourself unable to make a single decision without her. You cannot understand how you find it hard to make the decisions that your friends make easily.

Our relationship with our mother is our most complex relationship as it has the most influence on us subconsciously. It's worth examining as it will shed so much light on thought patterns and behaviors we take for granted.

Transforming Activity (Workbook p. 19):

1. What about your relationship with your mother is good?

2. What frustrates you?

3. How can you tell her what you as an adult need from her?

Chapter 9

Daddy Dearest

It would be most helpful to complete your questionnaire on **page 19 in the Workbook** before you read further.

Most of us have an idea of what a father-daughter relationship should look like. Precious few get to experience that relationship first-hand.

Again, our relationships fall into one of the following categories:

- The absent father. Did he leave the family or was he there but not available emotionally? Did he work away from home, or did he leave everything except work and his own interests to your mother? Did you know who he was inside? Was there addiction?

- He was there for discipline, but not much else. Experiencing acceptance and encouragement from him was unheard of. He thought of himself as fair and saying those things for your own good, but you just wanted him to really see you and value you for who you are.

- Your dad was your rock and protector growing up. He encouraged you but gave you firm boundaries. He let you have an opinion and choices, but he let you have consequences for negative actions.

- You're an extension of his self-esteem. He needs you to be on parade to show the world how great a dad he is. As long as you're willing to fluff his ego, you'll have a great relationship. But the rules are his. And you know that your dad loves you for him, not for you. Narcissistic fathers will fall into this category.

- You're totally dependent on your dad's opinion and feel you cannot make decisions without his approval. He in turn leans heavily on you for everyday errands, especially if your mother is not around anymore. You may feel like you have taken her place in his life.

- You were sexually abused by your father.

Our relationships with our fathers will have a significant influence on how we see men. It will determine whether we think they are trustworthy. It will influence whether we will be fearful of being abandoned by men. Through our father's eyes we look at ourselves – this is how we imagine men will see us. Do we measure up? Are we invariably going to over-compensate to make up for us not feeling worthy? How much bad treatment will we take simply because we fear being abandoned?

If we're lucky enough to be treated by our dads like Princess Cheesecake, the One and Only, but with respect for our separateness, our entire view of ourselves changes. We expect more for ourselves, and we're faster to dismiss relationships that are toxic for us.

Wanting our father's approval is a normal desire for a little girl of any age. I remember how my father ridiculed people who have normal fear, so at the age of six I decided I wasn't scared of his pack of ferocious Alsatians. They didn't eat me, so there must be some truth to the notion that if dogs don't smell fear they will not attack. That experience of trying to impress my father meant that I couldn't connect to feeling fear. I didn't know that I had fear of abandonment triggers, because I couldn't recognize any feelings of fear!

Leoni decided she would have to be her two sisters' caretaker. Her dad told her as she's the oldest they were her responsibility. She had to make sure they were not bullied so she built herself a bulletproof, tough attitude. "It was excruciating to make friends, as I didn't let anyone see my inner world. I was longing for a relationship in which I was accepted. I didn't notice that my relationships kept on failing because my I-do-not-need-anyone attitude meant I was pushing people away. I had to learn how to let people see that I am not bulletproof."

Sandra's dad died when she was only eight. He was her hero. They had fun. He was one hundred percent on her side. She tried to recreate that relationship in every relationship she had. The problem was that she idealized him as she was too young to remember the very humanness of his nature. Like all people, he had flaws and made mistakes. "I only remembered that he was perfect, so no relationship ever matched up. I would dash for the door as soon as I found that a guy had flaws. I took any negative comment as criticism. Sometimes it was only constructive input. Sometimes it was simply his opinion. This happened in relationship after relationship after relationship. I was looking for a perfect dad to protect me, not a husband."

More from **Tara** who barely knew her father:

"I was at school all day, got home, did my homework and the smaller kid's homework with them, went to work for a few hours, came back, prepared dinner, got them bathed, dressed, fed and ready for bed. At that time my mother worked long hours. Our father left at six-thirty in the morning and didn't return until seven-thirty at night. We would just get up and go to bed when we heard his vehicle come in. He would go from work to the pub before coming home. He never came in and greeted us; he just left in the morning and returned after dark. We only had time with him on a Sunday if he was in the mood. Children were to be seen and not heard. Our mother worked on the principle that he gave his salary to her for us so the fact that we never saw him and didn't know him didn't matter. He supported us. She had grown up with an absent father who walked out of their house when she was four years old and never came back. She thought my dad was a model father. We had a roof over our head; there was food in the house; he didn't shout or beat us. She used to say he wasn't a saint, but a very good provider and we should be grateful. She did her best with what she had."

Tara and her siblings grew up with a dominant mother and an absent father. Her 'normal' example of a man was someone who was emotionally and physically absent and took refuge in drinking. She married when she was nineteen and soon had a baby. She needed her own safe space and own family for connection. The marriage didn't last as he wasn't a good provider. He broke the 'good provider' rule! Husband number two was abusive, emotionally unavailable and took refuge in drinking too.

We tend to repeat what we know, even when we've different ideals for ourselves, until we step off the Hamster Wheel by becoming aware of our patterns.

Transforming Activity (Workbook p. 20):

1. What have you remembered about how you were shaped by your relationship with your dad?

2. Are you using it in a positive way by raising your standards regarding who you allow into your life?

3. Or are you so filled with abandonment fears and lack of self-esteem that you're overly ready to compromise to keep someone who is toxic in your life?

4. Are you staying away from relationships altogether?

5. In which way can you improve your own relationship patterns by being aware of the patterns you're bringing into your adult relationships?

Chapter 10

Primary Care or Primary Damage?

We're influenced by a variety of people in our lives as we grow up.

Primary Caregivers – Grandparents, family, teachers, friends' families and add-on families

Perhaps a friend had a close relationship with her family. And it shaped your view of what relationships should be like. Maybe you were lucky enough to have had saving people in your life, who accepted you unconditionally, who motivated you and celebrated your talents.

But you also could have had family who preferred a sibling over you. That could have taught you that you'll never be good enough. Your parents may have been so wrapped up in their own dramas that you needed to be invisible to not add to their burden. You could have internalized someone leaving as your fault.

Your parents' relationship might have been the formative factor of your youth. It could be they pretended everything was perfectly fine, but you knew what the icy silences and the hissing and spitting behind closed doors meant. It meant you couldn't trust your judgment. When children know that something is not right, but the parents pretend it is, they learn not to trust their own judgment.

It may have been a house in which we didn't see that it was safe for individuals to differ from each other, in which we didn't learn that withdrawal is not an acceptable way for an adult to behave. In such a house we cannot learn conflict resolution.

Add-on families are more the norm nowadays than parents who stay together for a lifetime. Taking into consideration all the adaptations merged families must make, overcompensation by either or both parents is one of the most damaging behaviors present. A lack of clearly enforced boundaries results in children not feeling loved. It could also lead to immaturity, as they do not learn delayed gratification. In merged families, kids easily adapt to manipulation techniques as it's so effective where parents who carry around guilt are concerned.

Somewhere along the line we've to ask ourselves if this was true for us. Have we adapted manipulation to get our way? Because manipulation may get us results in the short term, but it's a sure way of creating resentment in a relationship. After resentment come all kinds of alienating behaviors: withdrawal, retaliation, punishment, rejection, guilting, blaming and shaming.

Rejection is another side effect of being part of a step-family. It could be that the step-family rejected your approaches (or you theirs). Alas, the bigger fallout is that a father often 'throws away' his original family once he formed a new family unit. The children that are left hanging in the original family are bewildered and they know deep inside that it's because they are not good enough. Younger children will blame themselves; older children could well turn into rebels if they don't have saving people in their lives.

In merged families up to four adults, four sets of grandparents and countless other family members play a role, as well as the siblings, step-siblings and half-siblings. Some of us are lucky enough to gain support and an extra family. Others are not that lucky.

Transforming Activity (Workbook p. 21):

List all the people who played an important part in shaping how you view life negatively or positively.

1. What made a difference for you?

2. Make a list of Saving People in your life.

3. How did they influence you?

4. In which way were you negatively influenced and by whom?

Carefully examine each of these people's contribution to your worldview and re-evaluate whether their contribution is enhancing your life or if it's holding you back.

Next use the space in your **Workbook** to write the life lessons you learned from these influencing people in your life. In the provided column evaluate how true that learned lesson is for you today. Should that lesson still influence your outlook, decisions and life?

Chapter 11

Our Life-Changing Experiences

In everyone's life there are situations which change the direction in which we go.

- It could be someone's death, divorce, relocation or serious illnesses.

- It could be changes in income.

- It could be words carelessly spoken.

- It could be addiction or war.

- It could be going to boarding school at an early age.

- It could be that you finally gave up on your family.

- And some are wonderful experiences! Your first fish or a great family holiday. Making a team or passing well in a subject you dreaded. A new friend. Overcoming a big obstacle. Working extra hard and succeeding at your goal. Your own puppy. Learning to play an instrument. Finding out you're good at something. Being validated by a teacher. Your first bicycle. Your first kiss…

Many of these will be circumstances outside of us. Some will be excellent experiences. Some will suck. We unknowingly take bits of all our experiences into us. Some will shape us into better human beings. Some will debilitate us. Some will change us forever....

Before the age of seven and twelve

It's said that who we are at seven is who we are as adults. It's certainly true for the unexamined life, which tends to act out our childhood learning. It's a scary thought to think that your inner seven-year-old is in charge of your involuntary reactions, your thought processes, your viewpoints and your decision making. The lessons we never forget are learned in trauma, hurt and loss. Thus, most of our unconscious reactions are based on fears of abandonment and vulnerability – the feelings children of younger than seven experience during such circumstances. Young children may even internalize these shaping feelings, fears and beliefs from seemingly harmless jokes: "We're going to leave you at the zoo with your brothers".

Between seven and twelve we're able to be more discerning with what we allow, but still find it almost impossible to blame or reject our parents. In painful situations our overriding feeling is often helplessness, hurt and loneliness. We don't have a name as yet for feeling invisible or rejected but we've already internalized not being good enough.

And then we reach puberty!

In puberty[6] our brain chemicals change, and we become able to judge our parents for the first time ever. Before that we would blame ourselves as not being 'enough' or being the cause of negative things. With the onset of puberty everything changes. Now we question our place in the house and in society. We can challenge our parents' morals, world view and emotional involvement with us. We're able to reject our parents when we recognize they're never going to accept us.

It's possible to distance ourselves emotionally from our primary caregivers if we understand that nothing we do will ever please them. We stop expecting and then we cannot be hurt. That becomes a lifelong go-to habit when we're hurt by what we view as rejection.

During adolescence we turn our hurts into being a Rebel, a People Pleaser, an Avoidant, an Achiever or a Perfectionist, amongst other type possibilities.

We made these decisions at a time when our available options (being a Rebel, being a People Pleaser, being an Avoidant or being an Achiever) were not balanced with an adult's right to choices. We repeat these patterns later in life, as that worked at the time. If you decided as a kid that you're on your own and need to grow yourself up, what choices do you have? We don't see that we now have rights, a voice and choices. There is every chance that you'll again distance yourself from loved ones in an adult relationship in which you feel you're not noticed or have lost yourself.

These are other typical behaviors we adopt during adolescence:

- Show them they are right – you're as useless as they think.

- Stop trying and act like a fluff-head – if you expect nothing of yourself and no one expects any great results from you, you don't have to feel inferior.

- Find yourself a surrogate family to belong to – that will nicely explain the baby at sixteen and the useless guy you cling to because once he made you feel acceptable. Or have an affair to fill that need for belonging.

- Stop feeling. Period. Running away from feelings doesn't make them go away. They sneak back to bite you in the butt as hectic over-reactions when you're least expecting it. You don't know that, so you keep refusing to have feelings.

- Make triple-sure no-one can fault you at anything. Perfectionism is a bitch. In relationships it plays out as someone having only 'have to's' and no 'sure, let's negotiate's'. It results in over-control on the one side, and resentment on the other side. But for a criticized child it's a way out!

- Be the best people-pleaser ever! Bend yourself to everyone else's needs and refuse to acknowledge that you have needs which mostly go unmet. This presents itself as having too many 'Yes, sure's' and not enough 'Hell, no's'.

- Be overly responsible and everyone's caregiver. It starts in childhood when you find yourself being not the daughter they are supposed to take care of but their caretaker. It continues in relationships when you have no expectation that you'll ever be supported and cared for.

- Be so good at what you do that you'll be able to take care of yourself – bulletproof and not needing anyone! It plays out as someone who pushes people away with her high walls and self-sufficient ways.

Complete your **Transforming Exercise (Workbook p. 23)** before you read further.

1. Make a list of all the griefs and losses you suffered.

2. Decide which hurts needs resolving and processing.

3. Writing letters never to be sent is a great way to resolve past hurts and grief.

4. Talk therapy is helpful, as are art, meditation, mindful movement classes and being in nature. (Talk therapy could be with a therapist or in a support group.)

5. Being in a support group is the number one transformational thing you can do for yourself!

6. Find one new activity or group you can join.

Life-Changing Experiences in Adulthood

Let us consider a few of the big and obvious ones:

Married to addiction

Addicts are intent on hiding things from you. Lying and stealing feeds the addiction in the end. Trust is eroded. You wonder if you're imagining things and lose faith in your perspective. You become hyper-vigilant. You scan for signs of the addiction. You try to prevent situations that will lead to flare-ups. You don't understand the loss of connection. Addicts don't work things out. You have lots of unanswered questions and are presented with unexplained time gaps.

It changes you. You feel guilty for failing. You think you must keep things together. There remains little that is joyous to you. You start reacting to the smell of alcohol. Or join in as you don't know how to handle it. Or over-work or over-gym or over-eat…

You lack self-esteem, so you sit in the puddle of addiction. When you grow your self-esteem, you can say "No" and ask for better for yourself. If not, you'll stay past the point of reason and try to fix everything in your next relationship too.

You're predisposed to be an enabler. Then you notice what you're doing, and you stop taking people's consequences away from them. You let them grow up.

Addicted yourself?

You start without coping tools and a way to handle your feelings. You spiral down until you hit rock bottom. At rock bottom you lose important people or your health or something very dear to you. Most of all you'll lose the trust of those you care about.

The lucky ones who apply themselves to finding coping tools and finding support use their addiction as a learning experience.

The rest are still looking for rock bottom...

Married to a womanizer

Your self-esteem is eroded to nothing. You blame yourself. You started out with a shaky sense of self, otherwise you would have said "Goodbye, good riddance" at the first signs. If you don't improve your self-esteem before your next relationship, you settle for someone who treats you badly again. If you're left as roadkill without any new tools, you run for the hills if someone looks in your direction. Or you eagerly let someone put you together. If you grasp that you're worth more, you make better decisions based on how well you're treated, respected and valued.

Married to a narcissist

You cease to exist, because there is only room for one ego. And it needs constant feeding. You're exhausted, you distrust your own worthless opinion, you're an excellent peacekeeper and 'smoother-overer'. You give up eventually.

If you get out, your lack of trust in yourself needs fixing. You fear your narcissist and make him all-powerful in your head.

You can end up being diagnosed with a variety of useless labels which does nothing to help you get back to being an-adult-with-choices and a-right-to-opinions. The unlucky ones get meds-upped and float through life as 'Borderline Personality Disorder' or 'Depressed'.

The lucky ones learn their own worth, find their voice and their "No" and build a new life for themselves.

Death of a loved one

I am not minimizing the impact of death on the life of those who stay behind. It sucks. It's supposed to suck. It will take time to get over. Grief is a process and one must go through it, not around it, to move on.

But some will never move on. They will wear their hurt like a scarf of importance. Some will feel too much guilt in surviving to let their loved ones go. Some will use their hurt to remind themselves never to open themselves up like that again. Some will completely ignore the grieving process. As if we could.

Those of us with true resilience understand that life happens, and we cannot prevent harm to ourselves or our loved ones forever. We know that a strong essential self is what will help us to live with the unthinkable and carry on with lessons learned.

Serious Illness

You're reminded of your mortality and you learn to make better choices for yourself. You apply better self-care, go for more check-ups, live healthier.

Or you use serious illness as another reason to be sorry for yourself.

Life happens to all of us. These are examples or big game changers. We've smaller ones all the time. We've a choice in how we look at our life experiences. We can use every experience as a learning curve, or let it keep us stuck.

Examining Our Formative events

As we grow up and right through our life, we're going to be exposed to circumstances, experiences and events that shape how we see the world and how we choose to conduct ourselves in the world.

Most of our learning will be done unconsciously, without our being aware that we're making little adjustments:

- In how we present ourselves to others,

- In how we judge ourselves,

- In our belief system about our capabilities and

- In entrenching habits that can either keep us stuck or propel us forward.

Lena remembers being in charge of the household since she was only ten years old.

"My mother was quietly drunk and unavailable in her bedroom. She had a 'headache' since the day my father left. I was in charge of my little sister and baby brother. My sister followed me everywhere and my brother would cry non-stop until I picked him up. We needed to eat and have clean clothes and I still had to do my schoolwork. The welfare came along, but I got wise and made sure my mother was sober on welfare days. I stayed out of school some days to clean everything! I thought it was my job to keep the family together! If it wasn't for a kind neighbor who sent food over regularly I don't know how I could have kept us fed and presentable."

- Lena was now an enabler who didn't tell anybody how she struggled to keep the household together because her mother was drunk.

- She had to be a little adult who took over care of an adult and the household.

- She was confused about her role and forgot she was a child. She knew something was wrong but the neighbors and her father and her aunt acted like it was normal that she ran the household while her mother had a 'headache'. She became hyper-responsible and very serious.

- During her sober days Lena's mother ignored the fact that an under-aged child had to take care of the house. No one mentioned it. The Pink Elephant was completely ignored. Lena learned not to trust her own judgment – if the adults acted as if everything was fine, she must be wrong.

- She became a midwife with a passion for caring for people. Her self-worth became centered in how she could be of value to others.

- Being scared was a luxury which Lena couldn't indulge. She had to be fearless.

Lena's story turned out better than one could expect, although she repeated the pattern in her marriage.

"Lucky for us my father and his new wife sent for us and my mother went to rehab. It's probably not surprising though that I had no boundaries when my husband turned out to be an alcoholic too. Through Al-Anon I learned boundary setting and found a support group that helped me focus on my own recovery. Today we've a stable life and great family, but I first had to stop repeating my childhood patterns."

Marcy didn't believe in her own worth. Her husband liked to have a project:

Marcy and her brother were shunted from family to family when her parents were struggling financially. ¨I was so young that I thought it was because they didn't want me anymore. I was terribly insecure all my life. My husband had to reassure me a thousand times that he still loved me and wasn't about to leave me. The only problem is that I eventually grew up and Greg didn't like me not needing him for everything anymore. He started helping our single neighbor with all kinds of odd jobs and I could see where it was going. We went for counseling just in time. We considered separating but realized how much we still cared for each other.

"During counseling we discovered how much of our outlooks were unconscious. As we change as people, we are supposed to negotiate new ways to be in our relationship. The greatest thing we learned was that we could be strong adults who find our own happiness. We need not fill each other up. The surprising thing was that we could find our way back to each other when we learned to respect and value ourselves."

When you value and love yourself, you stop needing external validation. Greg learned that he didn't need to rescue people to be worthy. Marcy learned to ask for help and support when she needed it, but that she could do wonderful things for herself. She is a fantastic cook who is now running an events business successfully. She learned to trust her judgment and her instincts and take great care of herself!

Some life events are obviously harmful to us, such as growing up in any kind of unstable, neglectful or abusive situation.

But what about events that get brushed over as too small to make an impact, or "They are so young; they will not remember"?

Let's look at **Nicci's** story:

"I couldn't understand why others' needs were more important to me than my own needs. I had no recollection of most of my traumatic childhood though. Therapy helped me open up parts of my childhood and as my memories started coming back I remembered the trip to the orphanage!

"My father was part of the church incentive that collected toys and clothes and food for the local orphanage. We were to attend the yearly Christmas function for the children and we were jumping with excitement as there were going to be pony rides and clowns and party food. My father had a serious talk with us three kids. I was only five or six years old. He impressed on us how little these children had and how fortunate we were and how we must let them eat first and go on the ponies first. We gave our Christmas presents to them and didn't get new dresses that year. And for the rest of my life I couldn't accept gifts. I simply gave them away. I did for others and had nothing. I suffered financially but couldn't help myself. I worked for a pittance for a good cause.

"Until I remembered! Now I help, but I have learned to take care of myself too."

What if I truly believe I had a great upbringing and an amazing life?

Thing is, you may have had a great upbringing. You may have been loved and cherished, but sometimes you block out something that had a profound impact on you.

What about events that were out of anyone's control – those things everyone just needs to deal with?

Growing up during a war or having to go to boarding school very young are examples of circumstances we cannot avoid. It's 'chin up and march on'. Adults may need to be intent on survival and doing the best they can, but children are not equipped to deal with these things. To make sense of it they become little adults. They take on too much responsibility at too young an age. They lose their sense of fun and playfulness. They look self-sufficient and it becomes a life-long habit.

Sometimes it's what didn't happen.

My youngest memories are all of me being alone in my bed, or being alone in the playpen, or being with my caring grandmother who looked after me often.

What I don't remember is being cuddly with my mother. Ever. And I have no way of knowing if it ever happened. But I think I would have felt connected, would have felt more known, more noticed for myself, and less invisible.

It's not something I ever consciously thought about, until I started working through my thought patterns and my triggers. It was slumbering there in the background – informing my outlook and my belief system about not being wanted and acceptable and worthy. Although I have managed through the years to build a strong external self-esteem based on my capabilities and achievements, it didn't take away what I unknowingly believed about myself. I had to open it up and examine it and discard it by replacing it with a more realistic way of seeing myself before I could heal my life.

My mother was a kind, caring, responsible person, much loved by everyone. We were just not a good fit. I don't know what happened, why she had a hard time bonding with me. I only know that I had unconscious beliefs from the lack of closeness and I had to unlearn those beliefs in order to heal.

Formative events are not avoidable. Even though we chose at the time to accept an event as a lesson or an influence in our life, we can re-evaluate if we still need that belief or if we can do better for ourselves.

At the same time there will be loads of good take-aways from life happenings, and those we don't want to lose. We do want to make sure we're in balance:

- "I have to take care of myself; no one else will." CHANGES TO: "I am a strong individual who has this incredible capability to take care of myself, but I am worthy of support, love care and connection in my life. I can ask for the things I want and need."

- "I am responsible for everything." CHANGES TO: "I am a responsible person people can depend on, but it's not my responsibility to be someone else's adult. People benefit more when I let them learn from their own mistakes and I don't have such a big burden to carry. I can also ask for support for my problems and it's a great feeling to be supported."

- "I am a very loyal person and once you have my loyalty it takes a lot for you to lose it." CHANGES TO: "I am a loyal person, but I am also willing to take better care of myself by stepping out of those relationships with someone who doesn't deserve my loyalty anymore."

- "I am the person people turn to for help as they know I will never say no if I can help." CHANGES TO: "I am happy to help others but now I know that it's my job to make sure that my own needs are taken care of too. Now I know when to say 'No'."

- "I am hard working and dedicated." CHANGES TO: "I will do my best with any task I undertake but I now know that good enough is good enough. I can take care of myself by not being a perfectionist who pushes herself and others to breaking point."

- "I don't need others and I am self-sufficient as I can withdraw into myself when I am hurt. I can choose not to feel anything." CHANGES TO: "I am aware that I need connection in my life, and so I choose the people I can share my hurts and fears with. I recognize that it harms a human being if we don't have contact with others so now I choose to make more connections and reach out. I now know that my body will protest if I squish down my feelings."

- "I am a rebel and proud of it." CHANGES TO: "I don't need to rebel against authority out of hurt anymore. As an adult I am now able and willing to ask for my needs to be met and I have non-negotiables because I have a voice."

Our good points born out of a need to survive challenging circumstances stood us in good stead at the time, but there comes a time when our survival mechanisms start hurting us. When anything has a 'too' in front of it, or we're hurting ourselves, it's time to sit up and notice.

Next complete the **Transforming Activity (Workbook p. 25):**

The process comprises of working through your Workbook, as well as using Part 2 in which you will learn new coping tools. This will provide you with enough understanding to make the above transitions beyond behaviors and outlooks that served you once but are now holding you back.

CHANGING THINGS

Chapter 12

Overcoming Challenges

No journey is without challenges.

Taking a look at expected and unexpected challenges will help us set realistic expectations:

12.1 Physical Limitations – Is My Body Coping?

Now is a good place to stop and reflect on your physical limitations **(Workbook p. 26).**

Post-Traumatic Stress Disorder (PTSD) can be overlooked if you have not had an obvious traumatic event for which you found help. More specifically, living in relationship stress for a long time causes Relational PTSD. It is only recently that research has been done on the effects of the long-term fallout of relationships gone bad, and the continuous negative energy, unhappiness and sadness that go with it.

Post-Traumatic Relationship Syndrome[7] (PTRS) is a trauma-based syndrome that affects "individuals who have been traumatized by physical, sexual, and/or severe emotional abuse within an intimate relationship. In PTSD, there is overutilization of avoidant coping, but PTRS involves the overuse of emotion-focused coping", as explained by Karen Rodman, Director and Founder of FAAAS Inc. She suggested that this syndrome be called Ongoing Traumatic Relationship Syndrome[8] (OTRS) if the affected person is remaining in the relationship.

From this we see that ongoing trauma, in which you're still soaking, causes a trauma response. You may also have experienced big shocks on your journey of discovery. That could have added to the PTSD. Feeling disassociated from yourself is the biggest clue here, as well as being unfocused and experiencing memory loss. It's devastatingly easy to be triggered into recurring bouts of PTSD and finding someone who specializes in trauma release is a worthwhile effort.

This explanation by Lisa Schwartz goes a long way towards understanding why it's so hard to recover from trauma without specialized support:

"The majority of clients suffering with PTSD experience some form of unresolved dissociation as part of coping with overwhelming or stressful situations. While many clinicians understand dissociation only in the context of dissociative disorders, there is a much wider range of trauma-based dissociative responses. These responses can be a challenge to understand, detect, and treat because they are so woven into the fabric of how individuals survive traumatic experiences, and how they respond on a daily basis to triggers, overwhelm, and stress."

Lisa was seeing that her clients experience a fear response to their own stories and memories that prevented their unconscious memories from becoming conscious, so that these could be processed to provide healing. As a consequence of not being sufficiently neurologically supported, trauma sufferers were going into overwhelm, flooding, having unconscious reactions to the trauma triggers and experiencing defensive dissociation. This prevented them from processing, recovering memory and long-term positive change. (In response she developed CRM[9] (Comprehensive Resource Model) to provide processing and realigning of trauma memories in a safe and effective way.)

In simple language – when you experience PTSD you feel out of your body with no handle on your emotions or reactions. You feel separated from yourself.

It's nearly impossible to engage in the excellent practice of meditation when you're experiencing PTSD, as your ability to focus becomes impaired. But you can do Tapping (EFT) effectively with almost immediate effects. You learn how to stimulate meridian points by tapping on them with your fingertips – thereby tapping into your body's own energy and healing power. This has an immediate and almost miraculous rewiring effect on the brain. Try and find a practitioner near you or try some of Nick Ortner's[10] online resources.

There could be another reason why your body is saying 'enough'. You may have been **overdoing it for way too long**. That bitch, Superwoman, and our perfectionist people pleaser may be the cause of adrenal burnout. I-have-time-for-everyone-but-myself-personalities end up feeling drained and depleted. The next thing to pack up from burnout and too-much-stress-for-too-long is our thyroid. The poor little thing cannot take a constant cortisol overload and you end up feeling like you have nothing to give to anybody and are left with no compassion for anyone. When that happens, our hormones are messed up. That means our whole system is messed up!

We will see it in how many antidepressants, anti-anxiety pills and sleeping pills we pop. We will see it in our low energy and our need for coffee and other uppers.

This is the point where I advise you urgently to take action to recover your body to an optimal state. You'll need all your resources to realign your life to get those things we all want and need. Going after love, connection, support, acceptance, being seen and being heard makes it so worthwhile! There is good news here. A better relationship (the result of applying the tools you find in this book) will result in increased happiness, bringing down your cortisol levels and increasing your serotonin and dopamine levels. The best solution is to work on increasing your happiness at the same time as finding health practitioners who can support you in your journey to optimized well-being.

Also, if you're over-medicated, you cannot feel. That makes it hard to do this work. I prefer natural alternatives and appreciate the brilliant homeopaths, naturopaths, chiropractor and other intuitive souls who have crossed my path and helped me feel like myself again.

I can now focus and think and do incredible things because I started listening to my body.

I cannot dispense medical advice, but I urge you to find the solution that works for you. I also use medical practitioners who are respectful of my wish to use as many natural alternatives as possible, but there is a place for well-considered medical science as well. However, if the only solution to fallout from emotional issues is to get you on antidepressants or anti-anxiety medication, I beg of you to get another opinion first or consider ways which will allow you to process your feeling when you're ready to. It's of vital importance for us to have access to our emotions if we're to process them.

We cannot medicate away our unresolved pain and our unprocessed hurts. We've become part of a culture that somehow thinks taking our feelings away from us is helpful. The deduction is that we should avoid feeling hurt, or sad or lost and that grieving is bad for us. These feelings are a natural part of life and can be processed over time by honoring them. Unfortunately, we've lost the mourning and grieving rituals that brought structure and community to our process of working through pain or loss. We can change that by deciding to acknowledge, experience and honor our feelings from now forward.

It's up to you to make the decision that is best for you. You can Google side-effects and cross reactions of the medication you currently take, and the negatives associated with taking sleeping tablets. You can ask for references from friends and investigate better options. Ultimately you're the only one responsible for your own well-being, for the choices you make and for what you allow.

Just be aware that your emotional presence is required if you want to make changes that affect your emotional life.

12.2 Overcoming Challenges – Resistance to Change From Where You Don't Expect It!

During this process it's helpful to understand our brain's natural resistance to change. Initiating change takes considerable amounts of energy from it. Our brain wants to conserve all its energy to keep us alive and breathing. It is reluctant to give up energy for emotional change. But when we change our negative outlooks and become happier people, our brain actually functions better - it just needs a determined effort to get there!

Since we were small, our brain has also been in the habit of making us 'forget' hurtful stuff as it thought it was protecting us and distracting us by letting us have pains and aches we could focus on instead. The reality is that we've to retrain our brain by applying a new attitude. We've to make room for conscious responses by stopping old habits.

Two of the most actionable ways to start reconditioning our brains:

- Going after new and different experiences. Even if you only begin by moving your entire house around, it's a good start. Try new hobbies, make new friends, learn a skill.

- Stop doing harmful things. It's much easier to start improving our lives by dropping habits than it is to improve by acquiring new habits.

(Find your free e-book about *habits you can drop* in the back of this book under *Resources*)

It helps if we understand how our biggest ally – the brain – could be holding us captive by controlling the unconscious mind with a lot of unnecessary startup programs!

Get with the new program, brain!

12.3 Overcoming Challenges – Being Stuck

We may find ourselves in negative space a lot of the time – so much so that it may feel normal.

It may even feel safe. That is called feeling comfortable being uncomfortable.[11] And sometimes we will remain in that space for as long as it takes us to get uncomfortable with being uncomfortable.

There is a big movement out there praising us (especially women) for being comfortable being uncomfortable! It has a lot to do with pushing ourselves out of our comfort zones to achieve more. This is not what we're talking about here. We're looking at being in an emotional space that is hard and painful. We've grown so accustomed to being in this space that we feel a sense of being 'safe' there. It's what we know. That however doesn't make it a good place to stay stuck in!

If you're remaining in a bad space for a long time, it's time to look at your reasons for choosing to remain stuck. You may argue that you'll not make yourself feel miserable on purpose, so it must be out of your control. But we're never without choices.

- Someone left you → Sooner or later you must learn to accept it and live your own life.

- Your childhood was terrible → It is over now. Now is up to you.

- Something terrible happened to you → You cannot change that. You can choose if you want it to define you or not.

- You feel unloved, unwanted and isolated → Who will change this if not you?

- You hate your life → What are you doing about it?

- Someone died → Eventually it's your choice to live fully or in misery. There is a time when you can become ready for the healing process.

We are never without choice.

Holding on to your hurts

What if you have resistance to letting go of your sadness and fears? That will definitely keep you stuck!

You may, like **Ariel**, think that it's a safe place.

"My husband's suicide devastated me. Our relationship was rocky, but we always made up and fixed things between us. We were all each other had until the kids came along. His parents are both drug addicts and my mother has done nothing but criticize me all of my life. It's 'your brother this, your brother that'. There is no place for me in her life.

"Tom had an explosive temper and was very fond of drinking. Things got out of hand when he was drinking, but otherwise he was a good husband who took care of the kids. I forgave him easily as he was so sorry every time.

"Now I find myself spiraling down into a hole I cannot get out of. It has been five years and the girls are getting older, but I still cannot believe he is not here anymore. We've so many anniversaries to keep. I don't want to forget him, and I want the girls to remember him.

"I date on and off but invariably I feel so guilty that I break it off. I cannot be happy when Tom is not here."

Ariel never had good self-esteem, so Tom became her family and her savior. Because she didn't believe in herself, his suicide left her without inner resources. It was easier to play down his self-destructive habits and forget the fights and the sleepless nights when he would disappear. In her mind she gave him god-like proportions. She constantly said to her girls: "If Daddy was here we wouldn't struggle so" and "If Daddy was here he would fix that water pipe".

As long as she doesn't acknowledge that he is gone she doesn't have to grow up and make decisions. As long as she denies that he was full of human mistakes, no man can live up to him. As long as she refuses to mourn, she cannot be hurt again.

But for now, the question is: is she truly living? Does she not owe it to herself and her daughters to move on, grow up and be happy?

The only time we're willingly stuck in a negative situation is when we have a payoff.

A payoff can be an embarrassing thing to share but try anyway.

- It could be a widow wallowing in her new status as bereaved long past the expiry date, as she found importance in her new status. She is being noticed, comforted and cosseted for the first time ever.

- It could be someone who is so scared of being hurt again that they would rather relive the old hurt and use it as a reminder not to be vulnerable again.

- Low self-esteem could be keeping someone from trying new things.

- Blaming a 'perpetrator' is a good excuse not to try and risk failing.

- Making one's happiness someone else's responsibility keeps one powerless, but it works when one does not know one is a capable adult.

- Not wanting to take a chance on a new relationship is safer because it scares those who fear losing that happiness.

You get my drift. If that is you, look for it. You'll find a payoff[12].

When you identify your payoff, you become ready to feel better, you become willing to get help and to make changes.

Transforming Activity (p. 28):

Examine your hidden resistance to change:

- When you stay stuck you may be trapped by your limiting beliefs or your lack of self-esteem, self-worth and self-respect may prevent you from changing your circumstances.

- You could also experience a payoff from staying stuck.

Make a list of what it could be.

12.4 Overcoming Challenges – Limiting Beliefs

Ingrid shares her core limiting belief, and the fear of rejection that results from it:

"As long as I can remember I have had feelings of not being good enough. Even though as a child I had more guy friends than girls, I have found that with 'bad boys' I can be myself and my silly side is acceptable.

"My ex-husband cheated on me throughout our marriage. When I found out, I blamed myself; I wasn't good enough, I wasn't pretty enough, I wasn't skinny enough. All the old feelings of not being worthy came back.

"The next long-term relationship I had ended the same: cheating. The old feelings came back again. I knew the relationship was over long before it ended. I thought it was better to be in a relationship than be alone.

"Since then I have dated, but normally not more than two dates. I without fail find something wrong. If it's someone I like he is normally a 'bad boy'. I then find fault with them and run away before really giving any relationship a chance.

"In therapy I discovered I'm scared of being rejected and abandoned by yet another person so now I feel safe when I date unavailable men.

"I also learned that I need to be accepted for my true self and not to hide part of me away. I am now trying to get past date six without running away, because then I would have a clearer view of the real person I'm with, and they would get to know the real me."

For Ingrid the transformation started when she recognized that she was acting on her lifelong belief that she wasn't good enough. That belief caused a deep-seated fear in her that once again she would be rejected. When you realize that you're indeed 'good enough', you start making better choices that fit with your new self-view.

Limiting beliefs are not a life sentence. However, an unexamined limiting belief will keep you trapped in ways and means that you'll not be aware of, as it will all happen in your unconscious mind.

All our limiting beliefs are borne out of survival mechanisms from a time when we were small and helpless. As an empowered adult you have the choice to re-examine these beliefs and transform them into beliefs more suited to the life you want to have. You can now let your scared inner-seven-year-old go out to play. You can consciously take over the reins.

As an adult you have the capability to let wonderful things happen when you're determined to change these beliefs radically. Keep in mind that some may be so deep-seated that you'll find it hard to change or to uncover them without support. Working through the questions and exercises in the Workbook is a self-empowering way to bring them to the surface.

A helpful trick is to pretend you're talking to your best friend. What would she say? Then talk to yourself in that same encouraging, supportive tone.

Fake your new beliefs until you truly believe them. Say them out loud. Act on them! It takes only six weeks of your life of doing it until they become natural and second nature.

Transforming Activity 1 (Workbook p. 29):

Check those that apply to you:

1. I cannot talk honestly about how I feel.

2. I cannot express my feelings.

3. My feelings don't count.

4. I am not important.

5. I can't trust anybody.

6. No one will be there for me.

7. My views and opinions are not accurate.

8. There is no time for fun or play.

9. Other people's needs are consistently more important than my own.

10. I am always to blame for trouble. If I was better, it would be better.

11. I am just not good enough.

12. I cannot ask for help.

13. I have to control everything. If I can keep negative things from happening, all will be OK.

14. It's my job to make everyone happy. I can do that by pleasing everybody.

15. The people I love the most are the people that cause me the most pain.

16. I am unlike others, and my family is different from other families. I don't fit into the world properly.

17. I can deny anything, also to myself.

18. The real me is not a person I want to show the world. I am not as acceptable as others.

19. I am fully responsible for the success of any relationship.

20. To be acceptable everything must be perfect.

21. It's not appropriate to express anger.

22. Loyalty is not negotiable; I demand it and give it unconditionally. It's more important than the quality of the relationship.

23. Nothing is wrong, but I don't feel right. Something's missing from my life.

Transforming Activity 2 (Workbook p. 30):

Now we transform the limiting beliefs that undermine us the most by choosing a course of action. (Read the examples below before doing the exercise.)

Example 1:

"I don't believe I will ever get support. I have to do everything myself."

Transform this belief by taking action:

Identify what you need help with. Choose at least two or three people you can ask for help. (Don't put the responsibility on only one person. People can be overwhelmed by their own hectic lives, which doesn't mean you're not important to them). Decide how you're going to ask for help. Don't offer something in return. Don't apologize for needing help. All people need help at one time or another!

Ask.

Accept gracefully.

You'll find that people actually enjoy helping others!

Example 2:

"I cannot express my feelings."

Self-Investigation:

Why do I believe that?

Will I ever get what I want if I don't express my feelings?

When did this start?

Who will ever understand how I feel if I don't tell them?

I get it! No one knows exactly how I feel except me! I am responsible for letting people know how I feel!

Now transform this belief by taking action:

Decide on the most important thing you need someone to understand.

Simply state that this is your feeling. You have a right to feel your feelings and your desire is for the other to know how you feel.

Don't expect a change or lightning bolts! For that to happen is another limiting belief that needs tackling. This time you simply want to understand that you can say how you feel, without expecting change or action. And that the sky will not fall.

Go on, try it!

The idea is to transform your life out of Hamster Wheel patterns one limiting belief at a time by finding one small, doable action that will have the power of transforming your rigid outlooks and your set thinking patterns into a more empowering stance.

12.5 Overcoming Challenges – Setting Expectations for this Process

We have expectations of how things will go when we finally see the light. It's a huge relief that we're at last getting the help we have needed for so long. We feel like we've been sleepwalking for the longest time. We have this fresh new perspective. We can start seeing that the way we used to think doesn't have to be where we're stuck forever.

But it doesn't work like that. OK, some parts of it do work like that!

We start applying our new tools and we're so excited about changing our world!

'Empowered' starts to become a word in our vocabulary!

When we test our new ways of being, we're sometimes eager to apply the changes but often fearful that we may lose the people we care about.

But we push through our fears and we start to get positive changes in our lives.

And then we get resistance.

- Maybe the people in our lives are not changing as fast as we are and feel bewildered as our communication fails to keep them updated.

- Maybe someone has such abandonment issues that they read different behavior as losing you or rejection from you.

- Maybe someone doesn't feel needed any more. It can be that our new, assured, assertive self threatens the loss of their source of self-esteem. If their self-esteem was based on how much you need them for propping you up, the new 'self-assured you' leaves them feeling less positive about themselves! Their abandonment triggers may kick in.

- Maybe someone is not willing to step into adult behavior as they don't have the tool kit. They cannot step into adult because they don't know how to.

Resistance may be linked to your communication style. You may still need to get better at listening and allowing other people's opinions. If you're taking care to communicate often and in healthy ways, resistance could have nothing to do with you – it may be the other person's unresolved issues.

Resistance is not the end of the world. You can explain yourself better through being willing to have difficult conversations, which we cover in detail in the last chapter. You can elaborate through writing. You can communicate through having a changed attitude.

But you can also communicate clearly by having boundaries and by acting on your consequences. (More on boundaries to follow.)

Resistance makes the recovery phase messy. If your old habits or outlooks sneak back in, it becomes tricky. It's a bit like a teenager learning how the world works, but with better instructions! You discover yourself and your real place in the world. You learn to take responsibility for yourself. You learn to ask for what you want. You build a tribe of support. You try new things and trust yourself more. But it's as messy as being a teenager, because that is one of the phases of development that wasn't successfully completed because of a lack of guidance, insight and tools.

During this phase you may need a translator in the form of a couples' counselor. It will make it easier as it will clear up misunderstandings in a safe place.

When you're new to anything in the world, you're not going to be perfect. You're going to stink at something. You'll need practice to get better. That is OK. It's how it is, and as long as you remain willing to stay in the process, your life will continue to improve.

Yes, you may lose some people in the process, but you'll gain far more. Who you're becoming and the benefits that come with celebrating your true identity become your compass. We start to be discerning about who we want to spend time with, and our expectations about the quality of our interactions increase. This doesn't mean chucking people out of our lives. This is about having improved relationships with the people already in our lives and about attracting better people into our lives.

The next **Transforming Activity** is waiting for you in your **Workbook on page 30**.

Chapter 13

The Early Warning Signs...
We Choose To Ignore

All relationships have warning signs. That is because no one is perfect. We don't need to run away at every red flag, because the solution is not avoiding people with warning signs. The solution is learning different behavior around danger points.

But we do have to start by being aware that there are warning signs, and that we may be ignoring them because we're so desperate for the relationship to work.

Wishing it so doesn't make it so!

When people show you who they
are, believe them the first time.

– Maya Angelou

Oprah took this lesson to heart as a new life skill. This is how she words it:

Remember this because it will happen many times in your life. When people show you who they are the first time believe them. Not the 29th time. When a man doesn't call you back the first time, when you're mistreated the first time, when someone shows you lack of integrity or dishonesty the first time, know that this will be followed many, many other times, that will some point in life come back to haunt or hurt you.

— Oprah Winfrey

Every woman I talk to who is finding herself moving from relationship to failed relationship has a pattern. The pattern is in having the same relationship with the 'same' man who is treating her the same way. And the pattern is that she operates in the same self-belief system, the same reactions and the same behaviors as before. Sometimes our pattern is obvious to us. Sometimes we focus on the obvious and don't see our own underlying pattern. This one was wrong in this way, that one did that, the next one didn't do this...

My own story was no different:

I focused on the lack of connection I felt in my relationship, but I conveniently forgot that it was that way from the beginning. Right from the start he didn't share his feelings, he didn't have boundaries, he didn't want confrontation. I never felt that he took time to find out who I was. I knew I was valued for how I looked and for sex and for sorting out his problems. But he wasn't interested in who I was inside or in what my thought processes and motivations were. Nor did he know how to let me in. I lived with that emptiness because the gift of total acceptance I received from him was more than I ever had from anyone.

The lack of connection was obvious when he entered a room and walked right around me without making eye contact. It was obvious in his lack of interest in my life and my passions. But we shared enough to make me deny a basic universal relationship need.

When we eventually, after twenty-seven years, started working on recovering our relationship, I finally knew that a relationship without emotional connection from both sides wouldn't work for me anymore. I asked to be known. I let myself be seen.

And that is what we're addressing in Part 2 – we're becoming aware of how we give away our power, how we don't step up to be our own adult and how we ignore obvious signs because we don't want to be alone. We ignore obvious signs because we want to ignore them. We don't take action as we don't know how to. We're stopped by fears of rejection, our fear of failure and our fear of abandonment.

Find your **Transforming Activity on page 31 in your Workbook**.

Chapter 14

When The Hamster Wheel Stops Working – Understanding Where It Went Wrong

I can hear you say, **"But it used to work,"** or "I knew there would be uphill battles, but we managed through it."

Sometimes it's: "**I don't commit easily** but this time I thought it would be different," or "I knew that I should have canceled the wedding from the beginning, but my parents spent so much money and then I was pregnant anyway."

Sometimes we're determined to make it work, **no matter the cost** to ourselves.

Sometimes we go on in **a good-to-bad relationship** for a long time. We become accustomed to the idea that we cannot change things.

But perhaps you're aware that *you're* **not attracting the right kind of partner** because you keep on having failed relationships.

Mostly we don't recognize our patterns and cannot change them because we don't know we can.

Molly met Mike through an acquaintance and they fell in love immediately. Molly knew that Mike grew up with his grandma as he lost his parents in a car accident when he was nine. She understood it was hard for him, and that financially things were tight growing up. She loved him because he was kind and hard-working and he showered her with attention.

"I knew that Mike needed a lot of attention, but that was fine with me. I had a happy childhood with wonderful parents and although we fought like normal teenagers, I have very close relationships with my brothers and sisters. I have a lot of affection to give! I could make up for the loss of his parents and knew that we would build our own happy little family.

"What was great was to feel I belonged somewhere of my own, and that I mattered that much to someone. I believed, in our family as we were growing up, that it was most important that we supported each other. All of us being involved made it function as a big, happy family. But I did feel a bit lost sometimes, as if I didn't know who I was outside of the family.

"Mike excelled in his business and opened more and more branches all over. He spent his free time training for triathlons and excelled. It was as if he needed me less and less, the better he did in business and sport.

"I started saying things like "You never have time for me anymore", which was true, by the way. I felt like I was getting lost in the running between branches and training and competitions. I was saying, 'Your business is more important than your home' and 'We don't matter anymore'.

"When I cried and said I missed him, he would try and make up for it by getting me expensive gifts. Well, I actually know his assistant was getting me expensive gifts. I started feeling more and more resentful and hurt and left out, like I didn't matter anymore.

"First I tried to work harder at our marriage by being the perfect mother and wife. I supported his functions and his charities and did the sexy nightie thing regularly. He was always tired and always chasing the next deal and forever canceling the weekends away and the date nights I organized. I was used to working on my family's happiness as a unit. Now I felt alone and abandoned.

"The more I felt hurt, the more I criticized everything. How he brushed his teeth, his driving, how late he came home... Without noticing, my tone changed, and my body language changed, until I couldn't recognize myself.

"He became less and less available. I eventually gave up, but our life was still working. Our children were doing well, our house was comfortable, I didn't need to work so I had a lot of time to pursue interests. It didn't make up for me feeling rejected and angry, but I managed to distract myself.

"Then Simon at the tennis club started paying me a lot of attention. First, he was only helping me improve my serve, then we started catching up for a quick coffee. I was telling myself it was innocent. Truth be told, I loved that someone paid attention to me. Here was someone who was happy to see me!

"Through some kind of miracle, I decided to get help from a counselor when I noticed that I was starting to plan my life around my interactions with Simon. Finally, I understood that I had other choices.

"Firstly, I had to learn to see myself as my own person and like myself for who I am, not what I do for my family. Then I recognized that I could find my own activities that fill me with passion and find fulfillment therein. The hardest was to tell Mike what nearly happened and finding out if he wanted to work on our marriage.

"I didn't know to put myself in my own queue, and that it's my own job to ask for the things that I need to thrive. I had to learn to set my own boundaries and non-negotiables and how to have a conversation in which I felt heard.

"Now my happiness is not dependent on how much attention I am getting from a man, but on how much I love and accept myself.

"We're still getting marriage counseling. We had to. It was a long way back to each other. I learned so much about myself and I changed so much along the way. Each time I conquered another mountain of self-growth we had to renegotiate the terms of our relationship.

"I can now honestly say I am a happy person. I took a jewelry making course and have my own small business making special pieces on order. As I am growing in confidence and not depending so much on Mike to make me happy, we're spending more time together as a family without having to have pre-scheduled date nights. I guess I am much more pleasant to live with!"

OK, now look at the sequence above that took place in Molly and Mike's lives:

He needed someone to belong to.

She needed someone to belong to.

They both were happy to fulfill each other's needs. He needed someone to give him a family in order to feel that the missing part was fixed. She needed to feel important and stand out from the crowd by fixing someone's belonging needs. She got self-esteem from being his fixer.

He needed financial security to feel safe and so was driven to succeed. He was determined to be in control of his destiny as his world was so rocked by his parents' death. He built a lot of external validation through his achievements and relied less on being filled up by Molly. Besides, he belonged to a family unit now! Mission accomplished and checked off.

He changed the unconscious rules of their commitment by gaining self-esteem. Now the balance was skewed as Molly didn't grow her own self-worth internally and he didn't establish other ways of connection.

She felt less needed and retaliated by guilting, manipulating and judging. Her abandonment fears pushed her to seek closeness continuously, but it was through guilting and manipulation.

He felt guilty, pushed away and withdrew – he had handy excuses to hide behind. He could simply work more to distract himself.

She gave up on her marriage and withdrew by not trying anymore and hiding herself in distracting activities.

She found someone who was willing to fill up her need to be noticed – who boosted her self-esteem.

Now let's look at another 'happy marriage':

Elsa got the message when marriage number three crumbled. Or more accurately, exploded.

She knew that in some way she was involved in co-creating relationships that didn't work. She just didn't know how. She was married to such obvious scapegoats!

"Here was this ultra-charming, sensitive, attentive man who turned out to be an absolute manipulator!

"My history should have warned me. I was madly in love with Johnny, who was husband number one. He was repeatedly involved in one scheme after another, wasting our money on dangerous investments and partying if he struck a good deal. He was enormous fun to be with, and so handsome to boot. Eventually I couldn't stand the constant dread that we were going to be penniless again and I moved out.

"Jeremy seemed to me to be the absolute opposite and that was why I fell for him. He was well-to-do and much quieter and low-key than Johnny. My only problem was that he would turn our entire life upside down without a moment's notice. I would get home and hear he had sold our house and we were moving to another part of the country in two weeks' time. Or I would get home and he would have sold my car in my absence because he got a good deal on it. Look, he was brilliant at business, and invariably made good money no matter what he turned to next.

"Unfortunately, he turned to our neighbor next. As it turned out, it wasn't merely kindness and helpfulness on her side after his back operation. I found the two of them in our bed one day when I arrived back early and that was obviously it. I felt utterly stupid for being so trusting and vowed that I wasn't going to uproot my life again for a man. I had been working for a plant hire business, so after the divorce I used my settlement to start a small plant hire business of my own in my new town. I became busy almost straight away and did surprisingly well. That was when I felt safe at last. No one was going to uproot me again against my will!

"My self-esteem was at an all-time low after husband number two. I felt like I was a mindless doll in these men's hands, and now I was rejected as a woman on top of that. I had no intention of getting involved with someone again but one of my regular clients kept returning week after week to rent a chainsaw. He must have cut a forest down. I told Clive I had no intention of moving again, or giving up my business for any man, and he had no problem with that. He slowly won me over and was of tremendous help in the business. Or so I thought. Turned out he was lining his own pockets and having a secret life on the side. The appointments and clients he was seeing were a smokescreen. I didn't see how extremely self-centered he was and how he managed to arrange everything so his comfort was taken care of.

"In fact, he moved his girlfriend in while we were still under the same roof under the ruse that she was his niece who needed a place to stay. I couldn't get him out of my house, so I had to sell it.

"My father was strict and fair but dependable. It was a traditional head-of-the-house upbringing, with my mother handing over the finances to my father. I guess I thought that is how it's done. With my third marriage I at last decided to take care of my own finances by running my own business.

"We were not encouraged as kids to make our own decisions; we had to follow the rules. I loved and respected my father, but we didn't have a close bond. I always had a vague feeling that I was a disappointment to him – maybe because I never heard a word of praise from him?

"I know that I am making bad choices. It's quite obvious to me now. But I don't know how to make better ones, so I decided it's time to get help!"

When you're faced with a situation such as this, you may be tempted to say, "This one was like this, that one was so terrible and number three turned out to be a con artist".

Or you can say:

- What did I do wrong?

- What am I allowing?

- Why am I making such bad choices?

- What can I change?

- What is it I am not seeing?

These questions give you back your power. When you ask these questions, you're in the driver's seat. When you see yourself as a pawn in the hands of damaged men, you give those men the power.

This is the actual pattern that played out here:

Elsa had an unidentified hole in her. She grew up without obvious approval or affection from her father. Her head knew he must have loved her. Her subconscious told her she wasn't good enough and invisible. She made her choices based on being seen by men who were charming and affectionate. What she didn't see was that behind this charming veneer was a hurt individual with master manipulator skills. All three men grew up in difficult circumstances in which they had to learn to take care of themselves from a young age. All three had attachment disorders behind their charming exteriors. All three were happy to take over her life and to manipulate her by withholding affection if she complained.

As Elsa didn't notice how fast she relented when they withheld affection, she stayed trapped in this situation until it became unbearable.

She didn't realize her craving for male affection stemmed from her distant relationship with her dad. She thought her mother was a bad example because she turned over money matters to her dad. Her mother made it look like it was the expected thing to do, but it wasn't the reason Elsa found herself being in bad relationships where money management issues played a key role. In her was a hidden belief that she would waste her money because as a six-year-old she was severely scolded by her dad when she lost her pocket money. She didn't trust herself with money, but that only contributed to her handing over her life.

Her real trigger though wasn't feeling good enough for her dad, and that made her fall hard for men who showed her approval. Once she felt that sense of connection and experienced being good enough, she complied over and over. She didn't want to lose that feeling of acceptance.

She also didn't learn that her wants and needs count, and that she has a voice. Having boundaries changes the flow of a relationship. It gives the other parties involved the option to investigate their impulsive natures, manipulative styles of communication and past hurts. If they care about you enough they can manage to work through these hurdles and change the outcomes. If they have integrity, they will want to examine their own flaws and contributions. The bottom line is that consequences give people a reality check: do they want to continue in self-denial or are they ready to investigate which fault lines in themselves need attention?

If you don't have boundaries and don't know how to communicate effectively, there is little chance that you'll be able to influence the outcome in a way that will create a healthy relationship.

Hamster Wheel Relationships have the revolving, always-the-same-argument with always-the-same outcome pattern in common but also differ depending on personality types and conditioned learning. Although patterns have many overlapping features there is no one-size-fits-all fight.

Take a look at this example of a Hamster Wheel Argument:

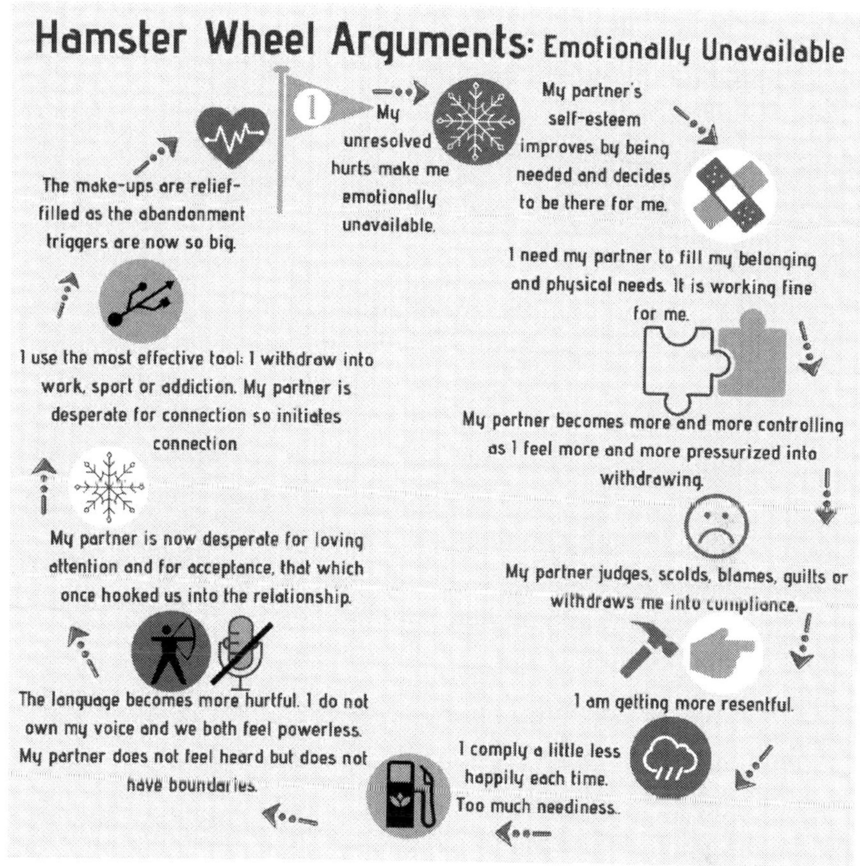

In our third example we see how we slowly give up our rights to our own life.

Leona is an incredibly talented woman. She is a gifted artist, kind and gentle, liked by all and adored by her children.

"After thirty-five years of marriage I have had it. We were typically young and in love and we did the normal thing. We got married, had two children, I went back to work when they went to school, and we bought a house.

"I didn't think much of it in the beginning. Everyone was doing the same thing. But times have changed and people around me are changing and my husband is still stuck in his ways.

"I never had an account of my own. He manages our money and insurance and things like that and he does it well. But I feel like I have no say in anything. If I make a counter suggestion or don't agree with him in any way he treats me to an icy silence for weeks on end or has such an outburst that I feel crushed for days. He is dependable and responsible and hard-working, so I feel mean about this, but it feels like I am slowly dying.

"My mother adores my older sister who looks exactly like her, and I was the one who looked like my father. It certainly didn't feel like she wanted me. I was little more than a toddler when she told me that I will have to be a very nice girl, because unlike my sister, I don't have the looks to keep a man. I blocked it out until recently! I have spent my entire life being 'nice' just to please my mother!

> "I don't want to be overlooked in my marriage any longer, but I have given up on him ever changing. Now I spend as much time as I can visiting my children and staying to help them for extended periods. It's a good excuse and easier than being home."

This is a version of **Helpless-and-Hopeless**, and this is how it came apart:

Leona has poor self-esteem as she wasn't accepted by her mother. She has been guilted and shamed into accepting a nice-girl-role. That brings you a lot of connections, friends and people who can depend on you. But it doesn't bring inner satisfaction and self-pride. Being 'nice' can bring a great measure of connection and affection which means you can carry on this pattern for ages. The price however is giving up your own self, your own dreams and your own aspirations. Other people's wants are habitually more important.

Her husband had a harsh father who instilled in his son that a man's duty is to provide a good livelihood for his family. He was continuously encouraged to do better so his family wouldn't suffer. His mother died when he was three and his step-mom wasn't cruel or unfair, just not particularly affectionate. He intensely dislikes being wrong as he was shamed when he made mistakes. Being crossed is a deep emotional trigger for him.

Leona's compliant nature charmed him, and while their attention was focused on building a family she managed to find excuses for his emotional distance. She did that because she was a nice girl, because she took it upon herself to fix what was wrong and because she wanted her family to look right in the eyes of the world and in her mother's eyes.

But underneath that 'nice girl' is a big silent fury at being disregarded for so long. She started being passive aggressive by doing things like not cooking his best-loved meal or by leaving a stain on his favorite shirt. She became rebellious in a very quiet way. She wouldn't do things that were important to him and then conveniently say she forgot.

She changed the rules by growing up and needing to self-actualize. She didn't communicate her new wants and needs clearly in a way that he could hear. Nor did she have a clear "No" as her mother's judgments were still playing in the background. Instead of having boundaries she withdrew and became sweetly hostile. She didn't step into being her own adult but blamed him in non-verbal ways.

He in turn couldn't pinpoint what was going on even though he could feel the difference, so he buried himself deeper in what gave him a sense of self-worth: providing for his family.

Leona's mother controlled her with guilt, withdrawal and anger, so it's easy to see why her husband's pattern continued to work on her. Until it stopped working. Leona wasn't equipped to continue her own self-actualizing though until she neutralized her mother's voice in her head.

"It came as quite a shock to me that I caused this whole mess. I never learned to stand up for myself! I was too scared to have a 'No' as I firmly believed he would leave me and people wouldn't like me.

"I had to work hard at learning to say 'No' and was really surprised the first time someone took it graciously! It was much harder to get through to my husband though.

"I think it took him by surprise that I wasn't moved by his angry outburst. I was shaking inside but I stood my ground and said, 'I am an adult and your wife and I have a right to an opinion.' And I kept saying it calmly until he could hear me. I think he couldn't hear me before because I didn't believe it myself. Because I didn't believe it myself I was almost apologetic and probably whiny – not a good place to have a self-empowering conversation from!

"There is still a long way ahead but so much has changed by my understanding that I had given away my right to self-determination and self-expression the first time I allowed it. I now see that I had the power all along to bring my opinion to the table. He wasn't a bad person trying to crush me; he was entrenched in his own patterns and his own story. I opened my own bank account and am managing it very well, thank you!"

Taking responsibility for the mess we find ourselves in has the ability to change our lives.

We do that in spite of clear and irrefutable evidence that we're in a relationship with an obvious guilty party. We take responsibility, so we can take our own right to self-determination and self-guidance fully into our own hands.

Here's another example of a Hamster Wheel Argument:

But sometimes we are the clear and obvious guilty party.

Vera took her first smoke when she was thirteen. Pretty soon she moved on to the green stuff, and it was a hop and a skip later before she raided the liquor cabinet. Her alcoholic mother and absent father made it easy.

It made her feel so much more able to handle things. The pain of abandonment was successfully squished when she was stoned and wasted. The constant bullying and terrorizing by the mean girl's squad disappeared once she started hanging with the 'dangerous' kids. She found acceptance in her group of misfits, but no acceptance was sweeter than what she found in the arms of Mother Marijuana. It became her safe place, her escape, her friend, her crutch.

She was simply not going to give that up!

Through a long and dangerous road which included getting expelled several times, flitting from sexual partner to sexual partner and running away from home many times, she managed by some miracle to get to adulthood, but not in one piece. She abandoned her studies, darted from job to job and from relationship to relationship. They were without fail older men who could care for her. But it never lasted. She moved on when there was the least suspicion on her side that they disapproved of her.

Finally, fleeing for her life when she was nearly abducted at a nightclub brought her to rock bottom. She got sober, but still boosted herself with a puff of green courage when she had to face a difficult situation. It was still her comforting mother – in her mind. She used all the usual justifications but the unconscious story was that she found her comfort there and didn't have tools with which to replace it.

Robbie was no different from the men she lived with before. Older, sensitive and supportive – like all the ones before him. But this time she was different. She was tired of running. She was longing for stability. And a child. She wanted a home of her own.

But Vera was her own biggest enemy. She still had her addictive personality. She still used her crutches.

"I couldn't take anything that sounded remotely like criticism. In the past I would just leave, but this time I was determined to make it work. But if I felt threatened or rejected or judged in any way I would instantly react. I would justify over and over, I would deny culpability, withdraw into hurt silence and feel so unlovable. I couldn't see the light.

"Robbie was amazing. He stuck with me through all of this. He had taken care of his entire family since he was sixteen and his father committed suicide.

"We had enormous blow-ups. We fought and made up and fought and made up and fought and made up! But he showered me with love. At long last I started thinking I may be a bit lovable.

"I started seriously working the principles I learned while in rehab. I read book after book after book and joined three support groups. Something got through to me and I started liking myself more. I learned that self-care was what I had to bring into my life and that I was worthy of happiness.

"Strangely Robbie became less and less loving the more I grew in myself. He took up woodworking as a hobby and would spend most of his free time in his workshop.

"I was so confused. I would go to group and feel excited and great about myself, you know, accepted and empowered. Then I go home and the person I most wanted to connect with brushes me off.

"The fights became bigger because now I was so very angry. I think the anger was smoldering beneath the surface, but I used to just drink it away. Now I was a spitfire the way my words flew into attack mode when I sensed he was about to leave again. I said unthinkable things. He did too.

"My turning point came when we somehow decided that we wanted a baby. I knew that I couldn't bring a baby into my messed up life. I wanted to do better than my mother."

So how did this come undone?

The writing was on the wall from the beginning. Vera didn't learn adult coping skills growing up. She started smoking weed and drinking at the age when we're supposed to learn how to transfer into the adult world. This meant she didn't learn how to function successfully in the adult world as weed became her 'problem-solver'.

Robbie grew up over-responsible. His father's teetering mental state made life at home unstable from when Robbie was a young age. He was his mother's rock and helped bring up his little sisters. He became a surrogate dad to them. He learned to be a very serious, very capable and very responsible fixer. He became an adult before he was supposed to. His childhood was lost, and he was caught in the Adult Child Syndrome[13] trap.

Vera needed a father.

Robbie needed a project. She was in in a relationship with an enabler, who for reasons connected to his own self-worth, had stepped into the guider/helper/savior role.

Vera started growing up.

Robbie lost his project. His self-esteem was tied to being the rescuer so when he felt not needed he suffered an ego collapse: What was his role and value in this relationship if Vera didn't need him to fix her? His deep abandonment scars made him feel that he was about to lose Vera.

Robbie withdrew into an activity that was distracting.

Vera felt rejected and unwanted and abandoned. She didn't have words for those feelings, but expressed her hurt as anger. The years of being rejected by her parents compounded the intensity of the hurt and anger concoction.

Robbie felt hurt by the criticism, contempt and personal attacks. The emotional blackmailing pulled him back in, but he became more and more helpless in the face of this new situation, so he withdrew into that which he felt he could manage and control – his workshop.

He started retaliating.

And the cycle gets repeated. Over and over.

This is the cascade of the Hamster Wheel argument:

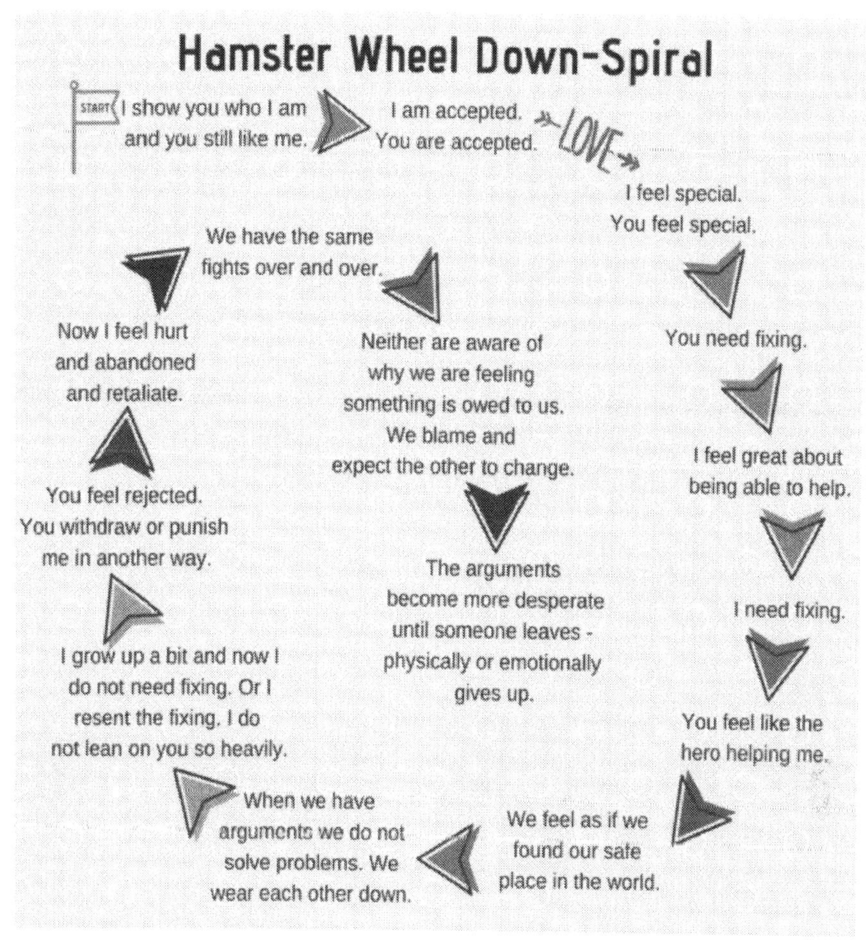

We go into relationships being aware of the obvious: how someone makes us feel.

If they make us feel special by showering us with love, attention and acceptance, we have adequate reason to continue in the relationship.

If we have self esteem problems and we find out that we're in turn needed, we find self-worth in stepping into being a fixer and filler-upper of another adult.

When they experience the same great feelings about being accepted unconditionally and showered with attention and they find something in us they in turn can fix and fill up, the scene is set for a co-dependent relationship that will work perfectly. It will start unraveling when one or both change the original rules of connection without negotiating new terms for the relationship.

Our abandonment triggers are mostly hidden from us. Our victim mode is invisible to us. Being unaware of our reactions to our hidden triggers lets us continue in destructive behaviors. Our limiting beliefs need examining in order for us to change into self-empowered and self-directed adults.

When you put two adults together – each with their own sets of unconscious behaviors and entrenched world views – they have a choice to mindfully work through these challenges and become more successful versions of themselves. Or they can slowly destroy each other and themselves.

Find your Transforming Activity **on page 32** of the **Workbook**.

TAKING YOUR OWN RESPONSIBILITY

I am only one, but still I am one.
I cannot do everything, but still I can do something;
And because I cannot do everything
I will not refuse to do the something that I can do.

– Edward Everett Hale

This is probably the most important sentence in this book:

> You are the master of your own life.

- No one else is responsible for your happiness, your life decisions or your consequences.

- It's not up to anyone but you to make you happy, fulfilled and complete.

- You're your own person. You're not attached to anyone else.

- You have the same basic rights as everyone else to joy, self-fulfillment, peace, self-expression, acceptance, connection and support.

- You're the only one who can do you, and you're the only one you can be. Go out and rock it!

Chapter 15

Why Do You Need This Relationship?

Problems don't go away.
They must be worked through or else they remain, forever
a barrier to the growth and development of the spirit.

— M. Scott Peck

Before you start reading, complete the **questionnaire** in your **Workbook on page 33**.

The questions are challenging but necessary if you want to free yourself from attracting the kind of relationships that you have been attracting up to now. It's better to work through these questions slowly and to come back to them again after reading this chapter. It will give you much self-insight and understanding if you do it diligently. Your answers may surprise you, but they will propel you towards better understanding and better choice-making.

(Evaluate all your previous and current serious relationships with these same questions. This will be helpful in establishing which core needs are causing the 'fatal attraction flaw'. Once you have identified a root cause, you can address it, neutralize it and replace it with more empowering outlooks.)

My need for this relationship:

- How does the relationship make me feel better about myself?

- What don't I have to face up to inside this relationship cocoon – even though it may be an uncomfortable cocoon?

- What does this relationship fix inside me?

- What do I gain from being in this relationship? List everything: emotional, material and practical. Someone needs to change the light bulbs, after all!

- What don't I have to do if I am in this relationship? And why is it important to me not to do this thing?

- What am I allowing?

- Where don't I have a "No"?

- For which adults am I taking emotional/physical responsibility?

- In which ways do I see myself as less?

- In which way does this relationship help me hide an insecurity?

- Where am I determined to get my own way? And why – how do I feel if I don't get my way?

- Can I admit wrongdoing on my part or does my limited self-esteem prevent me from ever being wrong?

- Do I only blame and bash myself?

- What negative beliefs does this relationship confirm about myself?

- How am I settling for less?

- Am I a perfectionist?

- Do you (or did you) self-harm in any way? If you did, where do you feel you cannot speak or will not be heard?

- What about this relationship is toxic to me, yet I don't acknowledge it?

- Where or when did I give up my voice?

- Am I able to accept someone else's "No"? Now be honest here! This is a hard one to answer. Are you more likely to explode or guilt or shame or manipulate someone into doing something your way? This may be an 'ouch' moment!

Your answers may have surprised you, even shocked you. These questions, no matter how painful to answer truthfully, have one revealing thing in common: They put you in the **driver seat** of your own life!

As we spend most of life – 70 to 80% of it at least! – being directed by our own unconscious mind, it's worth spending time finding out what the unconscious drivers and triggers are.

We give up our power as adults remarkably easy if we're not aware of our own triggers and limiting beliefs. The answers you uncovered here are what will tell you what you need to work on, what needs attention in your own life, where you can take your power back, and they will teach you what you're avoiding.

Part of becoming mindful in our own life and in our relationships is to start noticing the things we take for granted, the negatives we allow and the ways in which we give up control of our own life. We also need to notice our own triggers, our own destabilizing behaviors and our own patterns before we can change anything.

Before we notice these things, we will be in denial. This is another term I don't like to weigh someone down with as it sounds as if you're intentionally avoiding something. Rather, it is 'almost knowing'. Or not having language or tools so you stay stuck where you are – in denial. But never on purpose.

My Codependent Self

The questions above address the biggest reason we end up in Hamster Wheel Relationships: Codependency![14]

Codependency in turn is caused by our core insufficiencies – the hole inside ourselves. In the sections that follow we will address the root causes, our triggers, our outlooks and how to fill up our hole with self-love. We will work through it step by step, in manageable bites.

Codependents are without fail in a relationship with another codependent. Someone who is not codependent will not need fixing or propping up. They will not be willing to fix us or prop us up. They will expect of someone with a codependent hole inside herself to fix herself, take her consequences and be her own happy person, whether she is in a good relationship or not. Someone who is codependent will read that as 'not caring', but it will in effect be a healthy person applying self-care and self-respect to their own life. It will be another human being respecting you as an adult, but you may not understand it as such.

The questions above investigate our root co-dependent needs and habits.

(Next you can find a **Codependency Evaluator** in the **Workbook on page 37** to self-evaluate your own codependency score).

We can come back to both sets of questions as we progress on our road to a more empowered outlook and re-evaluate ourselves.

Mindfulness in Relationships

Mindfulness is a term we see everywhere, yet many of us fail to fully grasp what mindfulness means in a practical way in our everyday lives.

It may have its origins in Buddhism, but it's widely embraced by neuropsychologists.[15] Current research was made possible by developments in brain mapping. Meditation, our number one mindfulness tool, improves our happiness, health and well-being, but although I am a big fan of a regular meditation practice, this is not the kind of mindfulness we will be looking at here.

In relationships, learning mindfulness looks like this:

- **First Step** we experience a negative reaction. (It's any of the experiences described in *Triggers* in the previous section.) We know it's a negative reaction because it makes us feel terrible. Even if our heads are unwilling to feel something, our body will show a reaction that is not pleasant.

- **Next Step** we become aware that we're triggered by our negative reaction. It's anything from retaliating instantly to defending ourselves through justifications. It can be explosive, or withdrawal into non-communication.

- **Step Three:** We learn to PAUSE. Giving yourself a bit of space in which to stop your habitual over-reactions is one of the biggest gifts you can give yourself. It's also the only place in which we can replace our reactivity with a well-considered response.

It's very, very hard to unlearn our reactive habits. In the beginning we may still overreact. We may have to excuse ourselves long enough to go out, rethink things and find a better response. As we get better at it we learn to say, "Give me a minute, I need to think about this." Or to say: "I need to calm down if we're going to have an adult conversation. I would like to get back to you when I am ready to talk."

I find it helpful to remove myself physically if I am triggered and to go do a mindless activity like pulling weeds. But I also do put a time limit on myself. It's not fair to anyone to string things out too long, as anxiety tends to build in the people surrounding us.

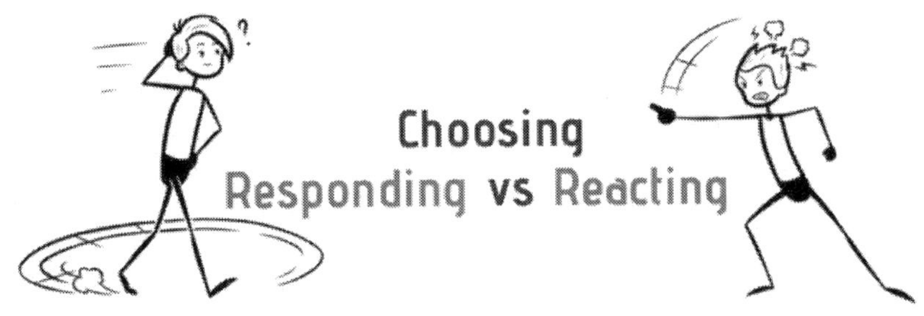

- **Step Four:** We **choose** a more effective and more appropriate **response**. While we're now in a space in which we choose to reflect on what recently triggered us, these are the two most helpful questions in the universe:

"What is this all about?"

And the next question resolves the problem:

"What is my hurt?"

When you're empowered by getting these answers you're in a position to ask the next crucial question: "What about this is my hamsters and my zoo? What about this is me allowing someone else to bring their emotional hamsters and their zoo into the mix?"

- **Step Five**: When you get the answer to these questions, you gain understanding. Once you understand you can choose a better response. When you are ready, you can go back into the situation that triggered you, because you can now neutralize your trigger.

- **Step Six:** Speak, but do so without:

  - justifying
  - blaming
  - guilting
  - going into victim mode
  - persecuting, or
  - retaliating.

If you examine your Hamster Wheel arguments for the above, you'll find your habitual ways of being inside an argument.

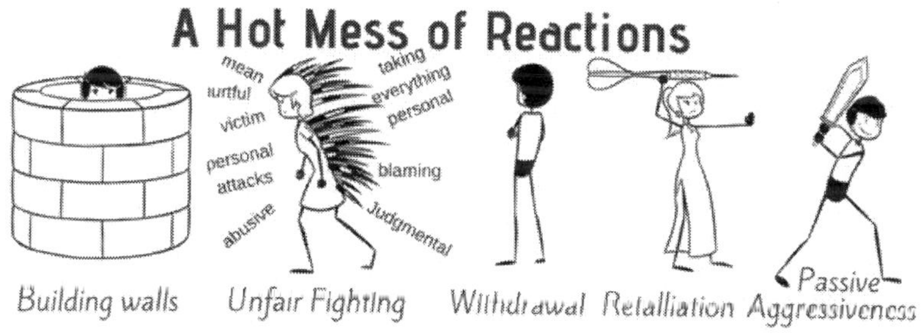

Building walls   Unfair Fighting   Withdrawal   Retaliation   Aggressiveness

We know the Hamster Wheel argument:

We know, word for word, what he will say, and if you say this, he will say that, and then this or that will happen. Every time.

Every time!

Until you're locked into the never-ending battle about nothing but about everything. And you cannot remember the beginning or untangle where you are now.

So, speaking out is needed, but follow the ground rules for effective communication:

- Accept the other's point, even if you don't agree or like it. Accepting that someone has a right to a point is quite a grown-up thing to do! So is telling them you respect their right to a view.

- Don't decide for them what they feel or mean. Ask.

- Clearly state how you feel, without guilting, blaming, judging or justifying. "I feel my input is not important to you when you don't let me speak", not "I feel you're an idiot for believing that!" "I feel unimportant", not "I feel you should listen to me."

- Negotiate a way forward.

(This is the simplified version, and we will delve deep into difficult conversations in the next section.)

PAUSE

P   Pause: Just stop. Do nothing. Excuse yourself and go to the loo.

A   Ask: Ask yourself what it is all about.

U   Understand: Understand that you are having a reaction but do not need to react immediately

S   Speak: Convey your feelings, your needs, your boundaries.

E   Exit: Do not stay locked in this space for days or weeks or years. Resolve problem points as they happen.

So to summarize mindfulness in relationships:

It's pausing long enough to understand your own triggers and finding better responses in place of habitual reactiveness. It's also pausing long enough to understand that the other person's reactiveness has nothing to do with you, but it concerns their own triggers their own hamsters and their own zoo! (You don't fix their part though, you just gently let them have their own responsibility).

When you have paused long enough to recognize your trigger, you deactivate your habitual reactiveness when you get the answer to the questions "What is this all about?" and "What is my hurt?"

This allows you now to choose an appropriate RESPONSE – not a reaction. A response is not an emotional reaction to someone else. It's a considered approach in which you ask for what you want and need by clearly stating your needs and boundaries without demand, judgment, blame, guilting or victimhood.

Joanna and Jake were masters of the Hamster Wheel fight. They had only three recurring fights, but it caused so much discord that they were barely speaking by the time Joanna came to see me.

"Every fight we ever had was about religion, his daughters or how much time I spent with my family.

"Jake is not particularly religious, so each Sunday is a tense affair, even before I open my eyes. I try my utmost to be kind and forgiving and filled with spiritual joy, but it's just so hard for me that Jake is not honoring his commitment for us to be a family who goes to church. His two daughters follow his example, and now they also refuse to go.

"That puts me and my children in a separate box, and that is the last thing I wanted. My two are now also getting rebellious, so I don't know how to handle the situation. Although I decide week after week that I will be gracious and tolerant, before I know it I snap about all sorts of things.

"This brings me to my second frustration. Jake's daughters were not easy, but before we were married we didn't see them that much. Now that they are studying here, it makes sense for them to stay with us. Jake finds it impossible to have any kind of boundaries with them. He says the divorce is hard enough on them; they just need love for now. In the meantime, they are turning into brats who get everything they ask for.

"The atmosphere is so tense at home that I spend as much time as possible with my parents. They have health issues and deeply appreciate the little things I

> do for them. Lately Jake has been making remarks
> when I go there about me having a home of my own.
> But that is it; I don't feel like I have a home of my own.
> No matter that he takes great care of my kids and me,
> I feel like a visitor."

For Joanna and Jake every argument started with one of them making a snide remark, the other one getting defensive, and the blame-denial-justification cycle started.

It needed just one of them to step off the Hamster Wheel and to start asking "What is this all about?" for the never-ending fight about anything and nothing to stop.

The problem was that the fundamental hurts and issues were not addressed, so their entire relationship got so tinged with resentments that arguments happened as if by spontaneous combustion.

The question "What is this all about?" got the same answer every time: "I don't feel as important as your daughters" or "I am not important to you or you would know how important it's to me to go to church together." The next was to ask: "What is the hurt?" This time the answer was that Joanne believed deep inside that no man would ever stay with her because her dad abandoned the family when she was nine years old. Next, she acknowledged that Jake's lenient behavior wasn't because she is not important to him, but because of his feelings of guilt towards his daughters because of the divorce. When she stopped blaming and justifying she could hear that he was willing to go to church with her, but on alternate Sundays. She didn't know that he felt his lack of time for hobbies was not important to her.

They agreed that Jake and his girls would go to family counseling to restore the balance in their relationship, and tensions lessened. Joanne no longer used the smallest excuse to hop over to her parent's house.

It only takes one person to become mindful for a relationship to start improving!

Summing up mindfulness in relationships:

- You take the driver's seat by finding out your triggers.

- You neutralize them by understanding what it's all about.

- You choose to take responsibility for your own happiness by learning you can ask for what you want and say what you don't want.

- You decide to take action in a mature and non-emotional way.

Identifying Triggers Is Whose Responsibility?

Becoming mindful helps all our relationships. That means firstly becoming aware of our triggers:

- What makes me angry?

- What makes me retaliate?

- What causes my throat to constrict and my heart to jump out of my chest?

- What makes me withdraw?

- What makes me mean and punishing?

- What makes me initiate relationship repairs even when I know I didn't cause the rift?

- What makes me settle for less?

- What do I fear most in my relationships?

- What makes me feel vulnerable, open and exposed?

- How do I define 'unfair'?

When we know what makes us feel terrible (all the above, right?), we can work on getting the things that will make us feel great:

- Connection,

- Acceptance,

- Being seen for ourselves,

- Having a voice, and

- Feeling supported.

When we're working on finding a better way to deal with our triggers, **the first thing to do** is to decide to stop reacting the same old way.

The second is to be aware that our triggers are linked to unresolved hurts and unconscious fears. These fears include fear of abandonment, fear of rejection and fear of vulnerability. As these fears surface we react instinctively to protect ourselves in the way we've been conditioned to. Dr. Rick Hanson calls these reactions 'paper tigers'[16]. It's a useful analogy, as you can train your body to relax by saying, "It's not a real tiger. It cannot kill me; it's just a paper tiger."

As we learn these triggers during trauma, they are stored securely in our primal brain, the amygdala, where they are out of reach for logical thinking. When the trigger presents itself, the amygdala flares into action with our conditioned response. The good news is that logical thinking, located in the frontal cortex, switches off the over-reaction. Logical thinking includes examining our triggers and analyzing our reactions by using our improved toolset, not our old reactive instincts.

Detachment from the triggering emotion

Once we know what our triggers are, we can choose to:

- Not react, or

- Delay reacting, or

- React differently.

We're **not powerless** over our triggers. Once we've identified them and chosen a better way of action we can get off the Hamster Wheel!

Now do the **Transforming Exercises (Workbook p. 37 to 40).** You're ready for it!

Use the Workbook to work through your triggers mindfully and plan conscious, effective approaches.

Chapter 18

Emotional Maturity, Anyone?

Surprisingly many adults don't understand that they are in fact, adults. Sometimes we get stuck in a powerless place where we've no awareness of our own right to self-actualization.

We're not aware that being happy, fulfilled and content is our own responsibility!

I have one key question for you if you're nineteen or older:

"Are you an adult?"

This could be a challenging concept to wrap your head around, depending on how you were brought up!

Now answer the questions **in the Workbook on page 41** to try and get an idea of where you are on the maturity scale. Give yourself a 1, 2 or 3 for every question (1 = nearly always, 2 = often, 3 = seldom):

1. I don't have names for my emotions and feelings. I cannot identify fear, guilt, sadness, joy, connection, remorse, admiration, abandonment, shame, happiness, etc.

2. I don't recognize when my stress level go up. I take out my stress levels on myself and others.

3. I expect of someone specific or other people in general to make me feel better.

4. I don't easily accept blame. I will defend myself fervently.

5. I feel very confused about being so reactive. I feel like I am on autopilot most of the time.

6. I don't feel as if I fit into the rest of the world. I feel misunderstood a lot.

7. I am easily controlled by either by someone guilting me or by someone's anger. Or both.

8. I make assumptions very quickly and am convinced that I am right.

9. I don't give others a chance to speak when I am upset.

10. I don't easily forgive and reconcile. I have a hard time letting go of mistakes.

11. I just don't get angry. Conflict is something I avoid at all costs.

12. I am easily offended and will either blow up or retreat.

13. I find it hard to assert myself.

14. I don't like exposing my feelings to others. Being vulnerable and showing how I feel inside is not an option.

(You'll find your scoring results in the **Workbook**.)

Understanding where high maturity scores come from:

If you were one of the lucky ones:

- You were encouraged to try new things.

- You were told it was all right to fail at things, as long as you tried and as long as you got up again. You'll possess more emotional maturity than most.

- If you were really lucky you would have been brought up with choices and consequences that were age appropriate. When you understand that you may choose whichever ice cream you want, but you're not getting another if you don't like it, and your primary caregivers stick to their consequence, you're lucky.

- If your primary caregivers hear and accept that you hate pink and don't like the taste of sugar, you know for the rest of your life that your voice counts. You'll most probably not be reading this book, as you will know to speak up for yourself, and that it's OK to walk away from that which is toxic to you.

- If you heard that your actions were not acceptable, but that you were absolutely always, unequivocally without exception, completely and utterly loved and accepted for who you are, you won't have to fill up the hole inside of yourself with anything or anybody. You won't have a hole inside yourself, and you'll like and accept yourself. Jackpot, sister!

How we were brought up will determine our level of emotional maturity. If our parents were not given the emotional maturity tools by their parents, they cannot pass them on. Most parents do the best they can, but if they themselves had limited resources, you're most likely experiencing the effects of it now in your relationships.

What to do if you scored average or low on maturity?

First, crawl out from under the rock you have been hiding under since you read your score! Low emotional maturity is surprisingly common. And this is a case of identifying the problem, so you can fix it and fly! Ignorance is not bliss – it's years and years and years of turmoil, loneliness and unexplained losses in emotional connection.

Do the best you can until you know better.
Then when you know better, do better.

– Maya Angelou

We don't get to where we are without learning something. If our life has been hard we learn resilience and perseverance. Sometimes the best thing to learn is that we've had enough and that we're ready to change what needs changing.

You'll be amazed and so impressed with yourself when you read to the end of the book, practice your new skills one by one and retake the maturity test.

The good news is that you can re-parent yourself! You can unlearn unhelpful viewpoints and damaging behaviors. More on that in the next chapter...

What exactly is an adult?

Defining it purely by age would depend on different societies, so let's go for somewhere between eighteen and twenty-one.

If we're to get technical, once you're out of school, studying or working, you're in the adult world and it's expected of you to behave like an adult.

The problem is what we based our concept of good adult behavior on! Or whom!

We're following the examples set by perfectly nice parents who were well-intentioned but often had a lousy upbringing themselves. If they didn't have a full toolbox they couldn't pass it on to you. If you were one of the unfortunates who had a challenging childhood, you're most likely going to struggle to be a successful adult.

The first reason is a childhood-development-basic-rule: A child has to complete each stage of childhood successfully to succeed in the next stages and to thrive as an adult:

Successful baby stage → Successful toddler stage →

Successful pre-teen → Successful adolescent →

Successful adult

If anything went wrong in your life during one of your developmental stages you likely are struggling to be a fully actualized adult. [17] Identifying your missing stages and completing them can be effectively done through re-parenting yourself.

Some of the disruptions to childhood development can be a parent temporarily or permanently disappearing because of illness or death in the family, frequent moving, harsh parents, unavailable parents, war, addiction or mental illness. It can be seemingly small issues like a middle child 'disappearing' in a normal family life or an overheard conversation. Until fairly recently the smell of smoke had the power to jerk me awake instantly. My subconscious tied smelling smoke to a classmate's house that burned down when I was nine years old.

Part of what happens during challenging stages of a child's life is that they turn into little adults[18] themselves. It could be a son assuming responsibility for the household to make up for his absent father and taking responsibility for his mother in her obvious distress. It could be an oldest daughter who is parenting her siblings because her mother is emotionally unstable. It could be the good little girl who knows not to aggravate her alcoholic father with crying or with other normal childhood needs.

The first big outlook adjustment to make is to embrace the fact that **adults have choices.** Children don't have choices. If you still see yourself as having no choice you have not made the transition into seeing yourself as an adult

The second important outlook adjustment is this: **You're not powerless.** When you're trapped in the powerless outlook you're trapped in a victim outlook: You believe firmly that you have no choice.

But this is what it means to be an adult:

- You have choice

- You have a voice and a "No"

- You have a right to self-determination

- You're not powerless. You don't have less power than any other adult

- You're willing to own who you are and step into your own skin and your own awesome path.

- You take responsibility for exercising your adult powers responsibly - not with force or coercion, but in a loving, affirmative yet decisive way.

Too many people live under the cloud of 'have to's' or 'shoulds'. Often it's self-imposed because they cannot see their own power, their own adult rights and their ability to make choices.

We may have the mindset of "I cannot leave this relationship because I cannot sustain myself financially". But notice the lack of taking responsibility for the choice made here. It rather is "I choose not to leave because it will be hard to sustain myself."

Here is another one: "I have to take care of my ailing father even though he is ungrateful and mean." In adult voice this is how it sounds: "Even though my father is not easy to take care of I am choosing to do it because I am a kind and forgiving person. I know that as an adult I can tell him his words are hurtful if I want to. I choose not to because his words no longer have the power to jump in me."

Being an adult is to see that your own power is in having choices and being willing to accept full responsibility for making a choice as well as for not making choices.

Your next **Transforming Activity** is on **page 42 in your Workbook.**

Chapter 19

Re-Parenting Yourself

Another characteristic of human nature
– perhaps the one that makes us most human –
is our capacity to do the unnatural, to transcend and
hence transform our own nature.

— M. Scott Peck

We cannot turn back time and do it over. But we can choose to re-parent ourselves!

The easiest way to achieve this is by following these steps:

1. Get a photo of yourself at any age between two and four years old.

2. Imagine a room full of preschoolers sitting in a circle. Look at them in your mind's eye, one by one. See if anyone was born unacceptable.

3. So you couldn't find one child who was born unacceptable, yes? Now add yourself to that circle as a kid. How about you? When you look at yourself as

another kid in the circle, are you somehow the only exception ever to be born without a right to be loved for who you are? How come you started believing that you're less worthy and less lovable? Less _______?

4. Decide that from now you'll treat yourself like all children deserve to be treated: with kindness, guidance, unconditional love and acceptance.

5. When you get to the point where you can make the connection that you're indeed worthy and born with exactly the same rights as anyone else, you're ready to re-parent yourself: You have the right to be unconditionally accepted for exactly who you are, with the inalienable right to a voice, to be heard and to be seen and to be celebrated for being the individual you are.

What if we have patterns that make us hard to live with?

This is indeed the point where we open up to the possibility that we may have acquired habits and thought patterns that make us hard to live with.

Our thought patterns influence our habits and reactions. Once we recognize that 'who we're born as' are utterly acceptable human beings without exception, we can begin to neutralize those reactions that drive wedges between us and others.

If we operate from unmet needs, unresolved hurts and unprocessed griefs, we're mostly acting in deeply entrenched ruts of over-reactiveness. The people we're in relationships with most likely have the same ruts to get out of. (We look at our behavior for self-evaluation, not for self-bashing.)

- It's hard to live with emotionally over-reactive people.

- It's hard to live with people who guilt you into submission in the nicest way possible.

- It's hard to live with passive aggressive people, who pretend nothing is wrong because they fear confrontation.

- It's hard to live with people who blame but take no responsibility.

- It's hard to live with people who take over your will and your life.

Are you 'those people'?

This is the point where we don't blame ourselves, but instead accept that we've done our best with the tools we had. We might have acted differently in the past if we'd known better, but we choose to forgive ourselves and move on. Who we are with our good points and our less than shiny moments is still a very human, one-of-a-kind awesomeness that is issued to each of us: acceptable and unique just the way you are.

This is the time to decide to accept ourselves as being born as awesome as everyone else, even though we may do things we don't like. Those are things we do, **not who we are** inside.

When we're only focused on the other party being the one who has to change, we miss an essential part of being a self-empowered individual. When we realize that fine-tuning our own behavior impacts all our relationships in an increasingly powerful way, we become excited about finding out where we went wrong.

Adult Child Syndrome

Growing up in difficult circumstances forces children to mature before their time. These children learn not to feel their feelings. They are overly responsible Fixers or Avoidants or Distracting Clowns, to name some of the patterns. Passives, Triangulators and Achievers are some of the other types. They lose their spirit of childhood joy and their sense of safety in the world. This is part of the Adult Child Syndrome.[19]

The traits of an Adult Child (AC) stand them in good stead growing up, but it doesn't work in adulthood. They have not successfully completed their childhood stages during which they should have:

- Developed a secure sense of self-worth and self-appreciation

- Separated successfully from their parents to develop as their own person

- Been taught boundaries and consequences

- Been respected for having a voice and a "No"

- Received acceptance for who they are, with negative actions seen as what they do, not who they are.

You'll find **Transforming Activities 1, 2 and 3 on page 43 in your Workbook.**

Are you an Adult Child?

Evaluate this for yourself by completing the **exercise in your Workbook on page 44**. We will address the areas where you didn't receive tools while growing up as we keep working through the next sections in this book.

Alana tells us how she found out she is an Adult Child:

"I am an alcoholic. There, I said it. It took me a long time to come to terms with that. I rather want to see myself as a good mother who made bad choices in partners. But through the Twelve Step Program of Alcoholics Anonymous I learned that I will heal when I become entirely honest with myself. My sponsor referred me to an Adult Child Anonymous meeting when I told her about my narcissistic mother and how I was abused until my aunt removed me from her care.

"My mother's entire life revolves around her and only her. I don't think she is capable of love or of feeling compassion for anyone else but herself. I tried for years to stay in contact with her, and just to get one real feeling from her, but eventually I gave up. I regained my sanity by severing ties with her and decided to see my aunt as my mother. It's less difficult.

"But it has not been easy. I guess the drinking started quite innocently. It was just a social thing, but it made me feel like the life of the party, and instantly popular, and so much easier to be around people. Over time I found myself drinking more and more and more. My first marriage sort of fizzled out. I was out a lot, and Bert didn't want to go out so much. So, we grew apart. My friends were not his. We didn't do much together. He was just too serious and quiet for me.

"I met Stuart rather predictably at a party, and we got married when I became pregnant. I stopped drinking for a while, as I genuinely wanted to be a better mother for my child than my own mother. But the socializing carried on. Loubeth was an easy child. She slept peacefully in her carry cot under the table even while we were out at a party.

"Stuart wasn't very dependable, but such fun. He did move from job to job a lot, so we moved regularly. Luckily, we had great friends and great times. It was tough too. We had huge fights, and he left several times but always came back. He cheated on me too, but each time I forgave him eventually. He was killed in a car accident, and for a while my sister supported me. At last she got tired of it and told me straight out that she wouldn't take care of me anymore, and that I was about to lose my daughter. That was when I knew I needed to grow up and start drinking less.

"It was only when I went to AA that I reluctantly accepted that I didn't just 'like' alcohol. I was dependent on it to get through the day. I needed it to even halfway like myself. I registered that I didn't want to be beholden to alcohol anymore.

"When I first went to an Adult Child meeting I didn't know what to expect. I was thinking: 'I don't have an adult child. What am I doing here?' I didn't realize that I was the Adult Child! I grew up long before I was supposed to because my own mother didn't take care of me. I had to be my own adult. I wasn't allowed hurts and fears because my mother's feelings were the only ones that counted. I had to stop yearning for her and be responsible for myself. In the ACA meeting I found that everyone else was like me. I thought I was the only one who believed I didn't fit into the world. Everyone else struggled with self-esteem and feeling acceptable and being easy around people. I found my tribe.

"Now that I am sober I cannot be with my old friends anymore. We've nothing in common! I can now have proper fun without needing a drink. It's different fun, though. I go to the park with Loubeth and we chase butterflies. We go to mother-and-daughter dancing classes. We paint and go to the museum and we laugh a lot. I guess I finally grew up."

Finding out that you're an Adult Child is a huge blessing. Seventy to eighty percent of the world population is walking around not knowing that they are running their lives on the coping tools they adopted as seven-year-olds, or twelve-year-olds. Even the most enlightened amongst us can benefit from becoming aware of our hidden triggers and conditioned responses.

The Adult Child program focuses us on the principle that we're in reality adults who can choose to re-parent ourselves with kindness, compassion and self-love.

It saved me.

Chapter 20

Dealing With Our Biggest Losses

When we get to the point where we look at the things we didn't experience as children and never will be able to, we experience our biggest losses.

We think that what we've had and lost are our biggest losses, but it's not how it is. Our deepest losses are what we dearly yearned for but can never have. These are what cause that hole in us we so desperately try to fill up with other things.

Say your mother died early. You sort of remember her, but you're not sure. You do remember her smell and her laugh and that you felt warmth and belonging when you think about her. You lose her to death and it's sad but there is a body to bury, other people who acknowledge your grief and the process of mourning. For the rest of your life there is support for having lost your mother so young. You have a right to grieve.

Now compare it with this:

You grew up with a distant mother who didn't accept you. She could have been passive aggressive and critical. She could have been reserved and may not have displayed affection. It could be she openly preferred a sibling to you.

You end up never feeling good enough. You doubt yourself and you make bad choices based on filling the hole inside yourself.

But you have no space to grieve in. You don't have a name for your loss and some doctor may label it depression. Your yearning goes unrecognized and your grieving couldn't start so it cannot end. You suffered a loss but your feelings are buried subconsciously. And for the rest of your life there is no support for your loss because as a child you had learned adult coping skills. You're soldiering on and that is what you let others see.

You end up never feeling good enough. You doubt yourself and you make bad choices based on filling the hole inside yourself.

This is what is meant by our biggest losses – that which we can never have.

A word of caution here: This is a good place to get support with the process. Here talk therapy is immensely helpful, whether it's finding a supportive professional or a support group. Writing is another way of processing feelings.

Be aware of feelings of vulnerability, feeling like a bowl of shaken jelly or behaving like a four-year-old, with emotions all over the place and tantrums making an appearance. These are natural parts of working through your newly remembered grief and assigning a place for it in your life.

This phase doesn't last a long time – from a few days to a couple of weeks usually – and with proper support and willingness to be present you can mourn your losses and process them properly and leave them behind forever. It becomes just your story and doesn't define you anymore!

Next you can go through this list in the **Workbook** and mark which of these you had as a child:

- Liked for myself and seen as an individual

- Unconditional love

- Nurturing

- Guidance

- Healthy boundaries

- Feeling safe/protection

- Feeling valued

- Acceptance

- Open communication

- A childhood spirit – a child being a child.

- A sense of contentment/peace/safety

- Intimacy in relationships

- Feeling good about myself/ positive self-esteem

- Support

- Validation

- Acceptance of my "No"

The more 'yes' ticks you have, the more you'll be equipped to make good choices for yourself based on a good self-esteem and an internal sense of knowing your value.

Unfortunately, the opposite is true too, and too often children fall through the cracks of their parents' lives. Their parents' own lack of tools turns their lives into turmoil and survival mode kicks in. For most children growing up in challenging situations, most of the 'yes' ticks are missing.

The list above also serves as our road map to re-parenting ourselves! These are the exact qualities and behaviors we want to identify and add into our lives.

The in-between cases are harder to identify.

You feel like you had a perfect childhood and may even say it. But something is wrong and your own life is getting increasingly messed up.

Bianca's story is an example of someone who had stable parents and a good secure home:

"I knew my parents loved me. I have a close relationship with my mother and my father was my hero. My older brother is a genius and an excellent sportsman, so he needed a lot of attention and carting around. My younger sister was acting out from childhood and we went through a rough patch when she had bulimia and later when my parents discovered her various addictions. The house literally came to standstill to get her through her crisis.

"In the midst of this I felt I couldn't ask for any attention. I knew I was helping my parents by not asking for anything. They had their hands full between Boy Wonder and Delinquent Sis so my problems were nothing compared. It wasn't as if I didn't need help. I was being bullied badly at school, but I decided to tough it out. Besides, I wasn't particularly brilliant at anything, just average, so I had to work extra hard to get good marks.

"My parents were super, though. My mom was going all out for us kids besides running a successful cheese-making business. My father was quiet and not demonstrative, but always stable and hard-working and kind. He wasn't the kind to show much affection, but I remember one incident clearly though. I was eleven and I fell down the steps and broke my arm. My father was the only one home and he at once rushed over and picked me up. He promised I would feel better soon and hurried me to the hospital. He was so comforting, like I had never seen him before. It was one of the best moments of my life, strangely enough.

"It was only much later during counseling that I managed to connect the dots: My frustrating marriage to a man who couldn't show affection, my selfless ways of asking nothing for myself, my frequent bouts of illness during which I lapped up the flowers and the undiluted attention I was getting.

"It was a dangerous road to be on, and I feel quite lucky to have learned that I have a right to my own wants and needs, and that I have a voice to ask for them. It's early days yet, and not everyone around me likes it when I am not so compliant and willing to do absolutely everything they ask me to do. My husband and I still have a long way to go, because he has to sort his own story out as I get clearer about my affection and support needs. But I am so much happier and more content since I recognized that I am essentially an empowered human being who can ask to have my needs met instead of being sick.

> "Looking at the road I was on scares me, because who knows where it would have ended. Yes, I still have lots of work to do on myself to fully settle into this new version of me, but it's so worth it!"

Having a 'perfect childhood' unfortunately is not a guarantee against slipping through the cracks and becoming an invisible child. Nor is it able to protect us from the lessons we internalize unknowingly.

Bianca's parents would be shocked to find out that their much-loved daughter resorted to being sick to get attention because she felt invisible unless she was sick. They may find out that their youngest daughter compared herself to her brother and inevitably felt inadequate and therefore needed to fill herself up with all kinds of addictions to fill her hole. The older brother now has burnout, and it may just be because he has a hidden belief that what he achieves is more important than who he is.

All of this in a 'normal home'.

Sometimes our minds play hiding tricks on us:

> The first thing **Penelope** said when she met me was, "I don't know why I am here because I had a very happy childhood."
>
> But Penelope completely blanked out a pivotal part of her history.
>
> "My father was my hero. I was tomboyish as a child, unlike my ladylike older sister. I did everything with my dad. I think he saw me a bit as the son he didn't have, although I didn't feel he needed me to be anyone else other than who I was. He was kind and

gentle and affectionate and my best friend. We hiked together, and I went to games with him. He came to support my tennis matches and cheered me on. He could do nothing wrong in my eyes.

"But when I was twelve years old, I heard my mother screaming for help in the room next door.

I stormed in with my sister right behind me. He was holding a gun to her head. We didn't even know he owned a gun! And here he was screaming that it was too hard, and he couldn't carry on and he was going to take all of us with him.

"Throughout the hysterical screaming and confusion and terror we were rooted to the spot until the gun went off, accidentally perhaps? Through some miracle there was just a click and then nothing. My sister stormed my father and we tried to wrestle the gun from him. The neighbors heard our screams and came in and pinned him down.

"An ambulance took him away. It was terrible. He was in restraints. I don't remember much after that. In fact, for years I pushed this entire incident from my awareness.

"It was easy, because the next morning we woke up and carried on like nothing happened.

We would visit him on Sundays in our Sunday best, crack jokes and eat our sandwiches as if it was an ordinary occurrence that your dad was in a mental institution. I don't think I told a friend or anyone about it. It didn't happen. End of story.

"Seven months later he came home and again we acted like he never left. That night was never discussed or even acknowledged. We carried on being a happy, cheery little family, intent on getting on famously!

"I never really did regain my trust in him, although nothing like this ever happened again. But having harmony in our house was more important, so that was how we conducted ourselves. Good little girls marching on.

"Is it any surprise that I repeated the happy-families-against-all-odds scenario in my own marriage? I pretended there was nothing wrong – until I fell apart!"

Unfortunately, 'looking normal' in the eyes of the world is what we learn from a young age, and families can behave in a relentlessly happy fashion if this is what they perceive 'normal' to be like.

There is nothing unclear about being in a situation where your father is threatening, and trying, to kill his entire family and himself. Yet we can push away the things that are too overwhelming for us to handle so deeply that they only become visible in other parts of our lives. Penelope has not slept a full night since that night, but only recently connected the dots. Like then, she has been intent on looking normal and playing at happy families without voicing her own needs. She fully believed that she'd had a happy childhood.

Family patterns are carried over from generation to generation. We become used to the way things 'should be done' and 'how we should look to the outside world' and we become convinced it's the only way. You can decide that it stops with you and that you'll start a new legacy by establishing a healthier family pattern in your own life.

The great thing is that with awareness we can choose to use these lessons to re-parent ourselves, and this time we can establish our own normal.

So, to get back to the list and how to use it to re-parent ourselves: when we look at what we ticked and what we didn't tick, the ones we didn't tick will clearly tell us what we can concentrate on.

When I first did my list, I was overcome by how little I counted. Because I wasn't brought up that way, I didn't count to me. I was nowhere to be found in my own queue.

It was only through finding affirmations, self-care practices and changing my belief system about my worthiness that I could fill the hole inside myself – the hole I expected others to fill. I learned I had the same inalienable rights to happiness, joy, fulfillment and connection that every child is born with. I understood that I am the only one who can be me, and fully accepted all my sides. I became self-directed instead of other-directed, which takes the feeling of powerlessness away.

Find your Transforming Activity on **page 45** in the **Workbook.**

You may not control all the events that happen to you,
but you can decide not to be reduced by them.

— Maya Angelou

Chapter 21

Self-Directedness Versus Other-Directedness

One of the best parts of changing our patterns is stepping into our own power. That means liking our opinions, our rights, our voice, our unique being and owning it. This is where you claim back the power you handed willingly to other people. No more do you need others to make you happy or allow others to make you miserable. You find your own batteries, you develop your happiness muscles and you become discerning about what you allow to jump inside you. Other people's opinions and judgments and anger become just that – theirs. You take on what you need, and the rest can pass through like a carnival visiting town. You can join in if you choose, or calmly watch them going by!

When we actively work on increasing our self-esteem it becomes easier to be self-directed. In turn, being more self-directed gives us more self-esteem.

Find your **Transforming Activity** on **page 46** in the **Workbook.**

Chapter 22

Emotional Intelligence

Feelings don't need to control reactions:

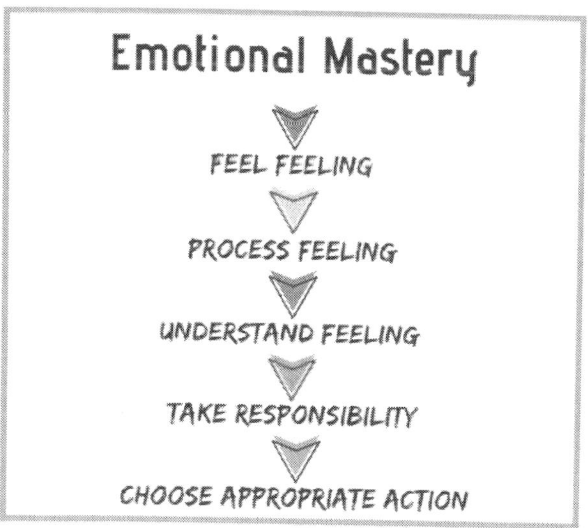

Emotional intelligence is becoming aware that feelings need not lead to immediate reactions, but that the logic of the frontal lobes can be used to determine the best response in the moment.

Emotional self-mastery[20] is achieved through:

- Self-management

- Self-awareness

- Relationship management

- Social intelligence

Anyone has the capability to learn emotional intelligence. It does require being available to our feelings though. Let's go through it step by step:

22.1 Self-Awareness

Self-awareness is the ability to take a good honest look at ourselves, our motives and our habits with total acceptance, but with total readiness to review and readjust our conditioned habits and our viewpoints.

The first half of this book focused on creating a better understanding of our emotional triggers and reactions. The aim is to achieve a higher Emotional Intelligence score.

A high Emotional Intelligence means that we're able to examine our immediate emotions, evaluate them and examine their origins and validity. This creates a pause during which our limbic brain's over-reactiveness is neutralized by frontal lobe logic reasoning[21] and we can respond from a non-emotional, logical, adult place.

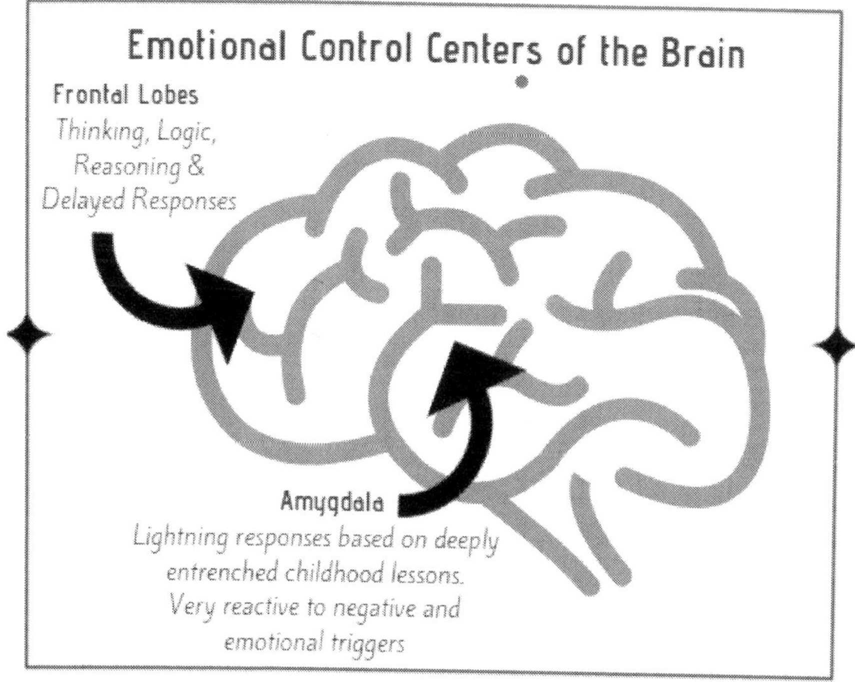

Having high Emotional Intelligence means that we're self-aware and can self-regulate in situations requiring social interaction, and that we can manage interpersonal relationships.[22]

The more self-aware we are in the moment, the more we realize that we indeed have the ability to stop over-reactions, control our responses and regulate our emotions. We achieve a distance from our emotions which means we process our triggers before we act. We find positive actions and empowering outlooks.

This is what the second half of this book is about:

- Self-empowering outlooks and behaviors, and

- Self-management through acquiring a tool set which includes flexibility in attitude and willingness to learn from our experiences and the people we connect with.

A key tool to start using when we set about improving our emotional intelligence and our self-awareness is to become friends with our emotions. When you're friends with someone you accept them, invite them in and are willing to learn about them. This is the way in which we tame our feelings: We don't judge a feeling as good or bad, we look at it. We don't refuse to feel a feeling, we invite it in, but not to live, only to visit. You get to know your feeling, but you don't let your feeling define you. You become choosy as to which feelings you want to allow in your life. You don't identify with a feeling: "I am feeling sad," not: "I am sad."

Feelings such as grief and sadness need to be processed in order for them to go away, but feeling rejected, powerless, shamed, not good enough or less than other people in any way can be reframed and turned away at the door as unwelcome guests. In their place we can invite in: 'feeling worthy', 'feeling acceptable', 'feeling lovable' and 'feeling empowered'.

Once we understand our emotions and have names for them, we can acquire the ability to accept them, reframe them or outright reject them. Some of us have suppressed our emotions for so long that we've no way of describing them or naming them. For times like this an emotion wheel is helpful. **(Workbook p. 47)**

Nissa stayed trapped in a lifestyle and a relationship that wasn't true to herself. She did what she thought was expected of her. She couldn't change her life until she became self-aware:

"I was raised in a Catholic environment, went to church, Sunday School and Youth Group and became a Youth Group leader. My life was built on doing what was expected of me.

"My parents divorced when I was seventeen and writing my final exams. I had protected the family at all costs because I was told growing up that I had to take care of my siblings. Well, not told so much, but if I didn't I was the one that got the belt or the back hand across the side of my head as it was my responsibility to ensure they never got hurt. I never did understand this but saw it as my role my entire life.

"Anyway, as a teenager I had a few relationships, both male and female alike. These never lasted. I was the one who would lay down the ground rules to start; it was on my terms we dated or not. I never had an open relationship with a female as this wasn't what good girls did. I was told that I would need to date and marry a good Catholic boy who would provide and take care of me.

"This made me want to run for the hills, as my parents' divorce was traumatic enough on us kids. I didn't want to marry and when my now-ex asked me to marry him I was caught like a rabbit in headlights about what to do. I tried everything, even down to telling him that I wasn't exactly straight and that I preferred girls to boys and that I didn't want children. This didn't discourage him. We started out married life all happy and like any married couple had our arguments. We had two children much against my wishes; however, I wouldn't change it for the world. They were the best thing to come out of this union.

"It wasn't long after we were married and settled that I started having doubts. Had I done the right thing? By all accounts I had because I'd married as I was supposed to, had children and was now settled. Hell no, I wasn't; I was being mentally and verbally abused, and would turn to other means to get me through these dark times: alcohol and extramarital affairs; again, with both sexes.

"It took twenty-five years for me to see that for the whole time I had lived a lie. I knew that I had to change something. This is where the guilt came in. Twenty-five years is a long time to be in a relationship and I had done what was expected of me. But why was I so unhappy? I tried everything; the obedient wife, the working wife, the wait-on-hand-and-foot-person, but nothing worked."

Still Nissa didn't have any tools to gain self-insight. She found alcohol a perfect way to drown her uncomfortable emotions. Extra-marital affairs provided a stop-gap way to supply the connection and loving she didn't even realize she craved. As often in life, it took a tragedy before she paused long enough to understand that change was needed:

"It took one horrific day that would change my outlook on life completely. If I hadn't hit rock bottom that day I would probably have ended up dead and/or remained in a marriage that was heading down the toilet.

"The incident that changed my life started like this. We got up and by ten am we were in the pub, doing what we did every day. Drinking had become my coping tool so that I wouldn't have to deal with my life. By four pm that afternoon I had had enough to drink, and a call came in about our dogs that had killed and hurt the neighbor's goats. The message given was not to let me come to the scene as it was very disturbing and that my ex should come. As per usual he passed it on to me and said, "You go and deal with it". Although everything was dealt with, I was sad and angry with too much alcohol in my system. I went down the neighbor's driveway and out onto the road. As I came round the corner past our drive I saw a truck coming towards me. I had nowhere to go. The truck that hit me was on the wrong side of the road and I ended up on the opposite side with a totally damaged vehicle. The police, ambulance and my friend tried to help me; however, being trashed, I refused any help. By now it was dark.

"In the truck that hit me were three men in the cab and on the back in the cold was a little boy. When the truck hit me, the child fell out. At the time I didn't know that I had had a hand in ending a child's life. In my argumentative, fighting and drinking mood I had to see − a sight that stays with me always. The father of the child and I were taken to jail that night. The sounds and smells are sobering. I sat on the thin mat that was to be my bed and just stared into space. That night I took stock of my life and realized that what I had done was inexcusable and right there I decided that it was time for a change. What the change would be I didn't know.

"I was placed under house arrest. I had to hand in my driver's license, ID and passports. When I got home I took a shower and went to sleep. After waking up I knew what I had to do. I could no longer live my life "the way I had been. I had had a light bulb moment in jail the night before. That was the last time I touched a drop of alcohol. Now five years sober, I stopped living my life as others expected of me. I live my life for myself.

"Left stranded by my husband when I told him that it was over, I was very close to hitting the bottle again. A friend stood by me through my court case and the dramas. She was my saving grace as she invited me to join her at an 'Adult Child' meeting. This was to change my life as I knew it completely."

We often only become ready for self-awareness once we run ourselves into a solid brick wall. It's because we choose to ignore the little warning signs on our way. Nissa was dreadfully unhappy, she escaped into alcohol daily, her husband left the decision making to her, she ignored her sexual orientation, and she felt trapped. Because she felt trapped she was passive aggressive and angry. She followed on her childhood learning by pushing most people away from her with her rejecting/defensive behavior. She was lonely and drowned her desperation.

Once we gain awareness of our driving forces and our limiting beliefs and habitual actions, we can decide how we truly want to live.

Nissa's story continues:

"I am now remarried, this time staying true to myself and not having any expectations of the other person. She has been an inspiration to me since I met her, and she remains an inspiration daily. What was different in this relationship and in this marriage is I don't need to change, I don't need to be anyone other than myself. I am accepted for who I am.

"My mom's words when I divorced my ex and told her I had met and was marrying another person and that this person was a female was: "I was wondering when you were going to be who you were meant to be". You could have knocked me over with a feather. My question was, "Then why did you allow me to go through with the first marriage?" My mom's words were quite succinct: "Would you have listened?"

"Now I know why I did what I did. Is anyone to blame other than myself? NO. I made a choice, but I didn't have the tools I have now.

"The only advice I can offer someone dealing with major issues: stop, get help, don't let others dictate to you how you should be. Just be yourself or the best version of you. Admit when you make a mistake, admit your part in the problem or issue."

Owning her true nature and letting her loving, softer side come out have brought her love, connections, friendships, better relationships with her children and even respect from her ex.

It's something that any of us can do.

Transformational Activity

Make friends with your emotions by using the Emotions Wheel on **page 47 in the Workbook**.

An identified emotion can be processed and changed.

An unidentified emotion subconsciously runs your life in negative ways

22.2. Self-Management

Self-management refers to the ability to rely on ourselves to regulate our emotions. We know the drama queen who takes over a room with her dramatized version of her problem that requires everyone's immediate attention as it's the end of the world. We may even indulge in variations of it ourselves.

I, for years, felt very sorry for myself because my husband couldn't make me happy! It became my focus, my only conversation and the determining factor in my daily happiness. It was an unforgettable day when I decided to at least try to decide how my day will be. And the day after that was better, and the next even better. I now get to decide how my day will be! I don't give anyone else that power – well not for long! When I do experience a negative emotion, which brings me down, I recognize it right away as it's not my habitual place to be. I evaluate it, see what action I need to take depending on how I contributed to the situation, and take action.

We have this daily habit of talking about our day and how we feel. The turning point was obvious the day my husband asked me how my day was and proceeded to answer for me that it must have been bad because he was in a foul mood. It astonished him when I said "Why? Your mood is yours. It doesn't determine how my day was. I had a great day!" I finally comprehended that I don't have to let anyone's mood jump in me, nor do I have to let anyone decide for me how I feel or don't feel.

Yes, I am simplifying, and it took determination to get here. But it's doable! I simply learned that my logical front brain had to evaluate feelings before I reacted on them. Switching off our old conditioned responses stemming from past hurts and deeply seated fears is indeed hard, but with dedication, awareness and support it's manageable.

When now we do succumb to reacting to negative triggers and soaking in it (and we will – it's a process...) we get out of it sooner by the exact same process: evaluate the trigger, reframe the emotion, see the habit that caused the downfall, and empower ourselves by stating how we're planning to do better by learning from the experience. (The habit that most often causes the downfall is 'making it about ourselves' – see the next chapter.)

Feelings follow outlook, not the other way around. We change our outlook, we change our feelings, we change our responses, we change our life!

If we're rigid in our thinking and outlook, we cannot allow the possibility that there is another way. It may take looking at your present way and determining if it works, before you get willing to try another way!

Find three great self-managing exercises on **page 48 in your Workbook.**

"Owl, you're just confusing things," I said.
"This is the day after Tuesday, and it's not Thirsds – I mean Thursday."
"Then what is it?" asked Owl.
"It's Today!" squeaked Piglet.

My favorite day," said Pooh.

– Pooh Bear[23]

22.3. Social Intelligence and Relationship Navigation

Both depend on one crucial factor:

Do you make every perceived negative thing about yourself?

You walk into a room and people stop talking. You withdraw into a corner, sure that they were discussing you. In reality Bonny just told the girls how embarrassed she is of failing her entry exams. They kept quiet in order not to further embarrass her.

Your boyfriend doesn't call you. You decide he doesn't love you and decide to leave him before he leaves you. His phone fell in the toilet and he couldn't call you until his finances allowed him to get another phone, but he was embarrassed to tell you of his money problem.

(No "Yes, but's"!!! Ask. Ask why he didn't phone. Don't assume. Don't decide for him. Hear his explanation and ask for more consideration next time.)

Your husband is not on time for an appointment. By the time he arrives you're passive aggressive. You feel he doesn't respect your time. He had stopped and helped at an accident on his way home.

(But it happens every time! Still, don't make it about yourself. Say you feel disrespected and that you would appreciate it if he takes your busy schedule into consideration. Tell him your relationship is important and that his need to be late is his own litter of kittens and his responsibility to sort out. Or that you'll appreciate a phone call so you don't worry.)

Sylvia's relationships failed one after the other, until she decided that she wouldn't make her feelings available to anyone again. No more relationships for her!

"I don't do relationships. It's too painful as date after date drops me as soon as they get to know me. It's easier if I don't let my emotions out. I love my job as a physician. It's enough for me and keeps me more than busy.

"I always rebelled against authority and I didn't enjoy the hospital environment, so I started my own practice as soon as I could. My staff is not close to me but do what I ask, so that works fine for me. I think they are a bit scared of me. At least with my patients I can be clinical and just do my job well. No emotional drama there.

"Most of my childhood is a haze. My father brought us up after my mother left with her lover. My father was bitter and switched off after that. I dimly remember him laughing and playing with us before she left, but that father also left. I tried very hard to get him to give me attention, but eventually I gave up. I knew that I wasn't enough for him.

"Against my will I fell for a colleague. I thought this time would be different as we were good friends for a long time. I don't know how we turned from friends, who could talk through the night, into bitterly squabbling enemies. The loss of this friendship was so potentially big that I finally became willing to look for help.

"It was only through 'he said, she said' accounts that my counselor could help me make sense of what was going on.

"Geoff is an introvert and when he needed quiet space to recharge I took it as a sign that he was going to leave. I felt unattractive. I decided I wasn't sexy enough for him. I believed I wasn't as witty as the receptionist or as charming as his last girlfriend. I made everything about me! I was so hypersensitive that every remark set me off into telling him how he thought I was terrible and unsuitable. I didn't see my own over-reactions at all. I was too hurt by what I decided he was feeling and meaning and not saying.

"I had to revamp my own outlook and did lots of self-esteem work. I had so much hurt inside me that needed to get out. I didn't even notice how I blamed myself for my mother leaving; how utterly rejected I felt by her.

"I fought my counselor every step of the way. I was so convinced that I was repugnant or something and would never be able to keep a man. But I got lucky or something. I stuck with it and tried the homework and exercises. This time I wanted to make it work because I didn't want to lose Geoff."

When you retrain yourself not to automatically make every perceived slight about you, you don't need to go into passive aggressiveness, outright anger, withdrawal or into punishment mode.

When you accept that the other person may have practical or emotional issues of their own, you can achieve enough distance to be reasonable and accommodating but self-respecting.

This is one of the biggest things you can do to improve your relationships forthwith and drastically.

Once you have achieved a neutral stance by not immediately over-reacting, you can apply your new skills and manage your relationships. You can give people a turn to speak, you can bring your own point to the table, you can be willing to negotiate.

Peace out!

Chapter 23

Withdrawing

Find your **Self-Investigating Exercise** on **page 49** in your **Workbook**. Be very honest with yourself, and explore which your own withdrawal habits are, in the space provided:

1. I started withdrawing long ago to protect myself from hurt. It worked then.

2. I cannot be hurt if I don't feel, so I will not feel.

3. If I let no-one into my life, I cannot be let down.

4. I feel a sense of power when I withdraw. It feels like at least there's something I can do.

5. I get a reaction when I withdraw. Someone tries to fix it.

6. The other person hurt me and needs to be punished.

7. I tried everything. There is nothing left to try. I give up.

Withdrawing has many triggers and the reasoning behind it could be any of the following, or combinations thereof:

- **You find safety** in being in total control of who you let in and do it very carefully. The wall is high and thick and will only be crossed by someone you have scanned repeatedly for signs that they may hurt you.

- **You'll let a select few in**, and only once they have repeatedly withstood your rebuffing behaviors and proven themselves to be accepting of who you are.

- **You bottle up your feelings**. You believe you don't need to feel during the withdrawing stage. It's not true, as we feel terrible during withdrawal, but it's what we've been telling ourselves for so long that we believe it. At that moment the deserted pain of withdrawal feels easier to handle than the pain that triggered the withdrawal: betrayal, rejection and abandonment. But withdrawing leads to a cascade of feelings that will eventually spiral down: hurt, anger, denial, grieving, loneliness, sadness, desperation, loss of hope, reactive outbursts. These can lead to a false diagnosis of Depression, Bipolar Disorder or Borderline Personality Disorder. These feelings can be experienced in any order, can recur at any time and will get progressively worse until Helplessness and Hopelessness are reached. Or if you're labeled by a well-meaning physician or psychiatrist you could be over-medicated and numbed out but still left with no life-altering tools.

- You believe **the world is not safe**. You don't trust people easily. You're too scared of being hurt again so you stay in your cocoon. You have been hurt so many times and so severely that your birthright of safety has been taken from you. You're traumatized and are experiencing PTSD. There are few people equipped to help you safely transform your feelings and even fewer will tell you that you can be re-triggered into PTSD if you re-experience your hurt triggers.

With de-sensitizing and re-aligning work like Lisa Schwarz's Comprehensive Resource Model[24] (CRM), you can heal. By processing your triggers mindfully, you can integrate yourself into society again. You can find safety in your own wonderfulness, in knowing that you're an adult with choices and in having a 'no', even if you don't know it and believe it as yet.

- Subconsciously you have learned that **withdrawing is a powerful tool that gives you what you need.** Someone in your life is invariably going to react to your withdrawing because of their own abandonment triggers. They will fix the problem by giving in to what you want. You keep doing it because it gets you compliance. You're not a bad person; you just have to learn that withdrawing is an unfair tool that will eventually erode your relationships. You'll learn that being vulnerable and asking for your needs to be met is way more effective.

- You're in a **near permanent victim mode** and believe that the world owes it to you to fill your holes. Again, you're not a bad person. You're someone who wasn't given the tools of personal accountability. You don't know the choice of taking your own initiative to self-regulate as it wasn't expected of you growing up. You only need to decide that you're an adult and your happiness is your responsibility in order for it to change.

Eliza and Jasper do the three-weeks-no-speak thing over and over. Both feel the other should know their feelings have been hurt. Both feel the other should automatically know what annoyed them or hurt them without having to say or ask for it. Sometimes they don't even know themselves what set off the explosion and the silent treatment. They stay in withdrawal mode until Eliza cries and Jasper relents and apologizes for he knows not what.

"Luckily I got tired of this. We've so much going for us but couldn't get out of this pattern. Through couple's counseling we've learned that mind reading is not an expected marriage skill. We both learned to ask for what we want. It's still hard, but we're both getting better at saying our feelings have been hurt or we would like support. It's sort of ridiculous for us to expect that the other knew what we wanted when we couldn't put it into words ourselves! Jasper especially is still struggling to identify his feelings, but we're both improving."

Transforming Activity (Workbook p. 49):

For every one of your withdrawing habits, write down a list of three or four alternatives you could rather try.

Chapter 24

Helpless – and – Hopeless

This is the point at which we examine the Helpless-and-Hopeless hole we can fall into if withdrawing and our lack of tools continues long enough. It takes a combination of things to end up there:

- You don't fully understand that as an adult you have **choices**, and that your being in a situation that makes you feel this level of dis-ease is also a choice.

- You're caught in a **victim outlook**. Feeling like a victim will lay a lot of responsibility on others – responsibility they may not be able, willing or equipped to handle. Or they may have been but are not willing to play along anymore. You too can become unwilling to be that person for others. We use guilting, manipulation, over-controlling someone else, blaming and judgment often when we're in victim mode. It may work for a while, until the other steps out of the game. When the other steps out of the game and refuses to fill up our unmet childhood needs, we've two choices: we can learn to fill our own holes or sink deeper into victim and despair.

- You have **codependent** patterns of entangling with others. You don't understand your separateness and 'function' best in an enmeshed romantic relationship and with only that one best friend that you also have a codependent relationship with: "I tell you my woes and you tell me your woes and we bash each other's enemies." You don't make your friend responsible for her own happiness by reminding her she has choices. An addiction to the person you're in a relationship with feels just right! You have no idea that instead of being addicted to your significant other you could be addicted to your own happiness!

- **Someone else needs to change** so you can be fixed. You hand the power for your happiness to another person who is also human, who has his or her own unfinished business, and is also responding to unconscious conditioning, exactly like you. You become more and more disillusioned and resentful and feel bewildered about the breakdown of your once functional relationship.

- You were simply **not issued tools** and don't know that there are tools available. You went to one professional after the other and think that you have exhausted the options.

- You're **tired** from the long struggle and **feel defeated** and without expectation. Your emotional resources are getting less and less as you **lose hope**.

This may be the stage where you reach out for help and the only advice someone has for you is to label you as being Depressed and to numb you with antidepressants. I hope it's not true for you, as antidepressants are not what you need in Hopeless-and-Helplessness. What you need is HOPE.

And here is the thing that gives you hope:

You're not alone in this. Many others feel the same way. You can learn to reclaim your power with the self-examination exercises and the transforming activities in this book. When you work through them, you acquire the tool set that gets you out of helpless-and-hopelessness. You may feel you have tried everything, but subtle communication nuances, self-esteem improvements and outlook adjustments change how you manage life.

I know, because I spent two years right there in the dis-empowered hole of Helplessness and Hopelessness.

There are days when only the Serenity prayer and holding on to that minute right in front of me got me through the day. One of the first things I did when I knew that I could not continue this downward spiral of self-destruction was to add to my circle of support. That and deciding to accept help when it came.

I think support was always around me. When we're resolutely focused on looking OK and fixing our own problems there is not much space for the angels around us to be part of our lives and our journeys. They are there; everyday people in our everyday lives, ready to help us if we become ready to ask for help and take help. People in whom you likely wouldn't have confided in before become part of your support system. Through hitting your own personal rock bottom, you can be vulnerable and show people your hurt. And unexpectedly strangers around you'll gift you kindness and empathy.

Melody found her way to the Helpless-and-Hopeless hole through years of having her non-negotiable needs for safety and a sober environment ignored by her husband. She tried keeping her world intact by being a perfectionist, outwardly in control of her life and appearing highly functioning – until she had to go home.

Big boozing parties, weekend after weekend and rambunctious friends partying nearly every night in her pristine environment eroded her sense of safety in the world. Her belief in her husband's love and support disappeared as he disregarded her pleas, her tears and her hurt.

Her safe zone wasn't safe anymore.

"Every day was like a silent collapse.

"I would leave my highly extrovert, high-profile job of megawatt professional output and Ferrari-type speed and then… Zero. When I reached home, I hit the kitchen door head-on, straight to Zero. My earlier 'Superwoman' capabilities in the workplace vanished and I crawled, magnetized, fell, and propelled myself onto the sanctuary of my bed. Depleted, exhausted, Zero. I curled up each day into a child-like ball, retreated into a soft, comforting blanket right up over my head and dropped off into the quiet and safety – the nothingness – of the craved blackness of Sleep.

"My life had no boundaries. I was terrified of confrontation almost to the point of regularly 'bolting'. I was reliant on a great need of approval and affirmation. My perfectionism was slowly poisoning my days. My emotional-heart was on the verge of 'flat-lining'. Dead. Zero. Absent. Yet physically I was Alive. So close and yet so far. I was skin-close to being an emotional corpse through the depression and hopelessness so perfectly hidden behind a smiley face. Even hidden to myself.

"Then I started to go to Support Group meetings and the long journey of self-work had begun. Understanding the dysfunction and the chaos. And the chance to improve oneself.

"As the saying goes, 'Life is a Journey' … and now I know with boundaries, vulnerability, self-compassion and building my inner self again, I will, dammit, enjoy the ride."

Melody found her safety in withdrawing armed with sleeping pills. She didn't know she had a voice. She didn't know that she counted. She didn't know that staying in those circumstances was also a choice. With support and insight into her own limiting beliefs and learned behaviors she could transform her life.

Find your Self-Examining Exercise in the Workbook: (p. 49)

Transforming Activity (Workbook p. 50):

1. How can you add to your support system?

Where do you need help? Identify and seek out friends, professionals, support groups and acquaintances that can help you with a specific problem.

No one person can fix everything for another, so making our support system as big as possible takes the pressure off individuals should they be experiencing a hectic day right when you need them. Having many options you can turn to means you continuously have support without laying your wellbeing on a single person's shoulders. Widening your circle of support effectively neutralizes the codependent habit of enmeshing with only one other person.

2. What are you reading? Where are you putting your attention? A friend suggested that I always have an empowering book by my bedside, ready to read should I hit a slump. It's what I have done ever since, and it's true:

Whatever we put our attention on will grow stronger in our life.

– Maharishi Mahesh Yogi

Crutches

We may have to let go of our crutches one by one! As we step into our adult selves more and more and practice self-actualization more and more, it will not only become easier, it will happen spontaneously. Our crutches may be over-involvement in other people's business, over-working, over-controlling, withdrawing, victimhood, co-dependent relationships, constantly looking for salvation through one modality after another, over-analyzing, intellectualizing, addictions, phoning life-line for every decision we need to make or chocolate! There are many more...

- You realize you're a **workaholic** because you find self-worth in your work. Plus, it distracts you from your problems. Now you change your thinking patterns and start saying "because I am worth it". Plus, you find help with your problems so they can be resolved easier. Before you were willing to kill yourself working.

- **You blow up** when someone disagrees with you and will defend yourself no matter the cost. You're a perfectionist who works hard at being right. You recognize your crutch is 'being valued for being knowledgeable'. Your self-esteem is deeply connected to that, so it feels like a mortal wound if someone disagrees. You fix it by finding lots of other things to love about yourself. You celebrate your successes and learn to truly like yourself. Now you're not volatile when someone disagrees, but you can choose to tell your viewpoint calmly.

- Or you're an Avoidant who **withdraws** into silence. You chose this habit at a time when you felt powerless, and now you're continuing your powerless outlook. You're also doing this as a punishment for the other person who is not giving you what you need. When you start to consider what you need, you see that it's a way of protecting yourself from further hurt because you've decided that you're not ever going to get support. But now you reflect on what this crutch of withdrawing gives you as a result: even less support, loneliness and isolation. Your health is suffering and you're constantly unhappy. It's clearly not working! You decide that you're an adult with a voice and that your happiness is your responsibility, so you may as well try to start speaking your truth and learn to ask for what you want and need – no matter how hard it is. You learn at long last that withdrawing is not safe or effective. It has only negative consequences for you and you hurt yourself most by withdrawing.

- You **over-analyze** everything because that makes you feel in control. You ruminate and do research and examine endlessly. You realize that you're focusing your attention on the problem, not the solution. You decide you want to find a solution, so you focus on getting help putting your research into action and not on doing further research.

We first identify our crutches, then find a healthy action to put in their place, then we give up the crutch. There is a place for going cold turkey, but relapse is more probable when the holes inside us are not filled and there are no coping skills in place of the crutch.

Self-Examination Exercise (Workbook p. 51):

1. Make a list of your crutches in your Workbook.

2. Look at which ones you're not willing to give up.

Transforming Activity (Workbook p. 51):

1. See what comforts your crutches provide

2. Find an empowering and healthier activity that will take the place of your crutch.

This way we can find the things that will make you willing to let go of your 'trusted companions'.

Chapter 26

Radical Acceptance Of Reality

We find it hard to let go of our crutches until we learn to accept 'what is'.

Byron Katie calls it "a lover of reality"[25] and further describes how our suffering is caused by how we think about situations.

When we change how we view the inevitable, our suffering goes.

'Radical Acceptance of What Is' changes our entire old outlook. It doesn't take away the grief and the loss, but it gives us a way of working through it, instead of resisting our feelings around the situation.

Beaulah and Harry have been married for 14 years. They got married young, their three boys are settled well at junior school and they are, by the look of things, a happy and successful family

Harry is not one of those men who shows affection. Everyone knows it. Yet he has been a stable, reliable husband all these years. And then seemingly without warning, Beaulah's life as she knew it disappeared.

"We've been the example everyone referred to as 'what family life should look like'. We ate together most nights, we went to church together, we spent many weekends hiking through new trails as a family. Yes, he often needed to be away travelling for his job for extended times. Even on those trips his daily check-in with us was non-negotiable for him. He made sure to talk to each of us every day and if there was a crisis, he was always our safe ground. Now I cannot make sense of it all. I don't know if it was all a farce, or my imagination that we were happy?

"If I really think about it, there were times when Harry was distant and absent-minded, but he didn't treat me badly.

"I was molested when I was eleven years old by a family friend, and although my parents supported me and I received counseling at the time, I always felt guilty around sex. It was fine by me if Harry didn't put a lot of pressure on me. We were best of friends and our children and our church community were everything to us.

"I sometimes think I dreamt that we had this beautiful life. I am all alone and shocked and angry and confused. And Harry and his Peter are happily running a restaurant in the vineyards.

What did I miss? How could I not know that he was bi-sexual? Nothing gave him away. He was head boy and an all-rounder sportsman. He was the apple of his god-fearing parents' eyes. Why could he not talk to me?

"How did I not know him?"

Beaulah's questions are normal and reasonable. These questions though are a sign of resistance and keeping her from healing. They are keeping her stuck in the hurt and the unfairness and feeling powerless over the situation. She remains a victim as long as she refuses to accept. She is not powerless though. Deciding to stop fighting 'what is' employs the logical brain and switches off the overly emotional limbic brain responses. Looking at what lessons she needed to learn further involved the logic reasoning frontal lobes, as did planning a course of action.

"I am now dating again and have expectations of finding a partner who is a better match for me. I now understand how compliant I was. I gave up my own dreams to create Harry's dream life. Yes, I was happy, but I did miss having a job. I am teaching again and I am loving it as much as I used to. In counseling I recognized that I needed to work through my sexual fears and shame. I am a work-in-progress when it comes to understanding that I can have a life in which I am fully present and enjoying being a woman. I now ask for what I want in relationships and can clearly say if something doesn't work for me."

When she decided to accept the situation radically she could look forward to building a new life for herself. She could help her sons through their own hurt and confusion and maintain a relationship with their father.

Which things that you cannot change are you resisting in your own life?

Transforming Activity (Workbook p. 52):

Write a list of all the things you have not fully accepted.

Next go through them one by one and find how the situation you resist benefited you. What are the lessons?

What were Beaulah's lessons? She learned not to ignore her gut feeling that something is wrong. She learned that communication between life partners is paramount for true intimacy. She never even told Harry that she was sexually violated! She learned that her own needs matter and that she is a person outside of the relationship and family life. She accepted that she couldn't change who Harry is or what his feelings are.

Chapter 27

Control

Over-controlling or being over-controlled is one of the most destructive patterns to be caught in.

Fortunately, it's also one of the easiest patterns to break once we're aware of what we're doing, or how we're being controlled.

First, we look at ourselves as the person doing the controlling. "Who, me? Can't be!!!" Or we know it, but in our minds, it's justified.

Let's ask ourselves these useful questions first:

- Do I feel like my partner needs me to keep him safe?

- Do I prefer to handle planning of most things myself, down to the last detail, and then prefer to do as many things on my list as I can myself?

- When I ask someone to do something, do I keep a watchful eye over proceedings?

- Am I quite critical of others?

- Do I often justify why I have to contribute so much based on other people's incompetence?

- Do I feel obliged to correct people?

- Do I believe I am always right?

- Do I struggle to say I am wrong or to say I am sorry?

- Do I like to have the last word in an argument?

The more 'yes' answers you have, the higher is the probability that you can call yourself an over-controller. I don't like labeling someone a control freak as that just make them feel guilty and wrong without empowering them with life-altering tools. Calling someone a 'control freak' will not make them give up a basic need to find safety through over-controlling people.

What helps is firstly to be aware of your pattern of needing control to feel safe and to prevent hurt to yourself.

If we learned during our formative years that being vulnerable wasn't supported and accepted, we give up on being vulnerable. In its place we learn to control and not to feel our own feelings. We establish habits that prevent hurt to our core self. One of these habits can be achieving a sense of safety by over-controlling others.

Over-control can often be justified.

My husband has ADD and is impulsive and used to be unsettlingly prone to freak accidents in which he injured himself. I had clear justification to be his eyes, his ears and his careful pre-planner. I had plenty of evidence showing me that he needed someone to steer him away from harm. I had to deal with the results of his impulsive actions many times. On the face of it my decision to try and prevent negative outcomes to him made absolute sense and was perfectly justifiable. I prevented negative outcomes to myself! If he didn't come to harm, I didn't need to nurse him, doctors' fees didn't need to be paid, production in our business wasn't lost. I didn't have to do so many important things by myself because he was incapacitated by some injury.

"But more than that, I had a fear lurking beneath the surface that he would kill himself by being impulsive.

Now that would be the ultimate fear – losing someone permanently. If that person contributes through a co-dependent relationship to our sense of self-worth and our place of belonging in the world, losing that person may be too overwhelming for the self to bear. We tend to push these same harm-preventing measures onto our children and our pets and all others dear to us.

The problem is that we exhaust ourselves by being in other people's lives trying to prevent negative outcomes.

So, the **most freeing lessons** to learn are these:

1. It is not our job to be another person's adult. If you are their adult for them, they don't need to become their own responsible adult. We will have to continue this pattern indefinitely unless we give others the chance to learn responsibility themselves. They may be surprisingly reluctant, as low self-esteem, fear of confrontation, fear of rejection and fear of being wrong could have kept them from self-determination all their lives.

2. We cannot control anything in this world except our own responses. We cannot control other adults (even though we try, because sooner or later they will grow tired of it, which will set the Hamster Wheel in motion). We cannot control world peace,

famine or wars. We can do our best everyday but ultimately, we've to let go of outcomes. We like to think we can take precautions that will prevent us from being harmed, but that is an illusion. I am not saying here that we should not be prepared, responsible, diligent, hardworking, caring or taking responsibility for our own part in things. What I am saying is that you can only influence things through your own involvement to a point, and there is a point where one can learn to gracefully let go of outcomes.

3. Having a Higher Power of your own understanding makes it easier to let go of outcomes, especially if we believe in a benevolent Higher Power. For some who have felt let down by God it's hard to believe in a benevolent Higher Power. We can also use the law of attraction to shift your viewpoint into hopeful anticipation. Having a more positive outlook not only helps us cope better, but it also almost miraculously attracts better people, better opportunities and better outcomes into our lives. There are many spiritual counselors and lots of excellent books[26] on the law of attraction.

4. Take a look at your own level of exhaustion. The more you're involved in other people's lives, the harder you work at running around preventing outcomes. The longer you try to be perfect, the higher your own levels of depletion will be. Allowing others to have their own outcomes may be disrupting for now, but in the long run it will result in your being surrounded by more people operating from an adult stance. When the people around you are in adult mode, relationships improve, frustration levels drop, and you can spend time and energy on your own growth and self-actualization.

Letting go of control over others is surprisingly freeing.

These are some helpful phrases you can try:

"I have full confidence in your capabilities to do this on your own."
"We all have to start somewhere. Just go ahead and do it. If you mess up you try until you get it right."
"I am sorry that I used to prevent negative outcomes for you. You're an adult and it's not my job to take away your consequences."
"Your way may not be the same as mine, but it's not up to me to tell you how to do things. I accept that you'll do things your way."
"Good enough is good enough."

Find your useful **Self-Examining Questions on page 53 in your Workbook,** and your **Transforming Activity on page 54.**

THE MISSING TOOLS

Chapter 28

Conquer Constant Anxiety And Sadness

Where focus goes, energy flows.

– Tony Robbins

I see a lot of women in distress who are caught in an anxiety/fear loophole or stuck in a regrets-and-what-could-have-been cycle.

Here are two questions for you to answer if that is you:

Do you experience a lot of anxiety? If the answer is yes, observe how many of your thoughts are focused on what can go wrong in the future and what you fear for the future.

And

Are you feeling incapacitated by sadness? If yes, notice how many of your thoughts are regrets and refusal to accept what happened. See if you can identify feelings of powerlessness.

Ruminating in the past with endless repeats of 'why', 'he should have', 'if only', 'I cannot believe she did that to me' or 'yes but' puts us in the **victim loop**. There is only one way for that spiral and that's down into a diagnosis of Depression and ending up over-medicated. And that is the way some may like to go. A diagnosis and medication lend validity and weight to your hurt, do they not? For everyone else who is done with being stuck in suckitude, keep reading!

Being focused on the past – and the regrets and sadness that come with that – keeps us in a place in which our bodies cannot recuperate from our loss. It puts unfair stress on our adrenals and thyroid, as our entire endocrine system is affected by our emotional state[27], and vice versa.

It keeps us feeling disempowered, abandoned, rejected, invisible and angry. Those are typical victim feelings. I am not questioning their validity, I am challenging their usefulness, because there is not a single useful attribute about being stuck in a victim state.

On the other hand, when we're constantly focused on our future fears, we're building up our own anxiety levels without having any positive effect on the future. The next obvious step will be anti-anxiety medication – and no access to your feelings again.

(A note: Panic Attacks are caused by our subconscious responding to a trauma trigger and may need professional intervention. They are anxiety in overdrive.)

Neither being **stuck in the past** nor **stressing about the future** is of any use to us. Here I am also not saying that normal worry about fear inducing situations doesn't require your attention. In fact, the opposite. Having your thoughts constantly in the future is not productive, as your thoughts are not actually capable of averting disaster.

But taking control of the situation by:

- Deciding if you can do anything about it,

- Realizing which part of the problem you can do anything about, and

- Finding a suitable course of action to make the situation better

is the most adult, most present thing to do.

The solution

Learning to direct our attention to the present moment is the solution for our sadness/anxiety loop. It's a practical and commonsense principle, once you get it. It's just not most people's habitual thinking pattern.

You can never have the past again.

Never.

You cannot change the past.

You can only learn from it.

You cannot ever be in the future. Go ahead, try.

Never!

You can only plan as much as humanly possible by using your past lessons.

And then you have to let go.

You can only ever be in this moment. Right now.

That is all you have.

This is where you're effective. This is where you have power. This is where you can take action and make decisions.

So amazingly simple, but so effective.

OK, I know it's hard. I had to unlearn my own bad habits and **learn to be present in my own life** too.

But it's possible, and I will share with you **a secret** that will make it much easier to retrain your thought patterns. Simply notice when you're feeling bad and redirect your thoughts to the present moment. Listen to your body; it will tell you what your state is way before your conscious thoughts recognize the triggers. If you pay attention, you'll observe a quickened heartbeat, constricted throat, dread in the pit of your stomach, nausea and for me, a pounding headache.

Transforming Activity (Workbook p. 55):

What are the sensations you feel in your body when you're unhappy, sad, anxious or triggered? Where do you feel it? If you squish your feelings, pay attention to what happens right before you go into auto-squish-mode. (Find more exercises in your Workbook.)

Our outlook and thought patterns keep us trapped, and they can be changed!

The only place where time is real
The only place where we can feel
The only place where we can know

– Elsa Mendoza

Remember that you can handle everything in the present moment, even if it's only because you have no other option but to find a way to handle it. You have already survived big hurts, difficult circumstances and serious loss. You're more capable than you give yourself credit for. Just get your butt out of the future and the past, as the present is the only place where you can apply your empowering new tools!

You lack nothing you need in order to exist
at this precise moment.

— Martha Beck

Chapter 29

What Is A Healthy Relationship?

People have different ideas about what makes a successful relationship. For most people it will include feeling safe, supported, connected, being peaceful, with very few fights and having some common goals.

There is nothing wrong with those ideals for a relationship. But that is not what makes a successful relationship.

A successful relationship is one between two whole individuals who don't need fixing and are not looking for a project. They know that the relationship between them needs to be constantly renegotiated because both will continue to grow and change as individuals and both are willing to do it. They both expect that there may be challenging times in which their partner may not behave perfectly as we're human after all. They both are willing to talk and to listen.

A relationship that is *not* based on this principle is based on:

- Our need for someone else to fix that thing inside us that is our own job to fix, and

- On our desire to puff up our self-esteem through being of value to another human being.

When we both arrive with healthy self-esteems:

- The need for being fixed by someone else doesn't exist, and

- The need to fix someone else to improve our own self-esteem also disappears.

-

This is new information for someone used to being in **codependent relationships**. In codependent relationships we tend to be enmeshed and acutely aware of which parts of ourselves we've to neglect to keep the other person near us – and the other way round.

We are in codependent relationships because a core need needs fixing and we're willing to fix another's core need.

In a **healthy adult relationship,** we're not there because we need to be, but because we want to be. That is a base for a much stronger and more respecting kind of union – respecting your own strengths and your own ability to have your own needs met through clear communication and having boundaries. In turn you're willing to respect your mate's capability to do the same.

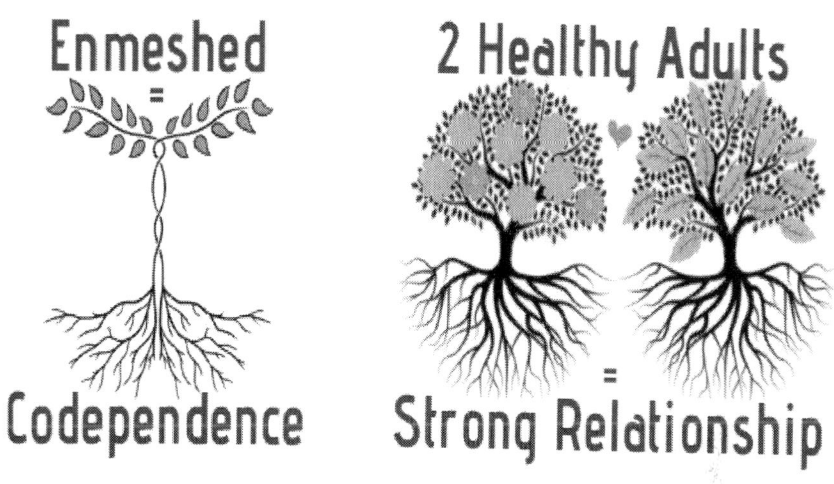

We' have to be aware of our **own subconscious resistance to feeling less needed** by our partner, especially if you feel that your usefulness has been an important factor in keeping you from being abandoned by your partner. If you identify and recognize this inside yourself, it's useful to note and park it into the relevant slot: a relationship based on what you can fix in your partner will eventually deteriorate until it may become unbearable for both of you. Let your partner be a strong person, secure in his or her own capabilities. That is the relationship you deserve – one between complete individuals.

As being in a codependent relationship is **the main cause of Hamster Wheel relationships,** it stands to reason that desiring a healthy relationship with a healthy individual is the first step out of repeating the same disastrous mistake over and over.

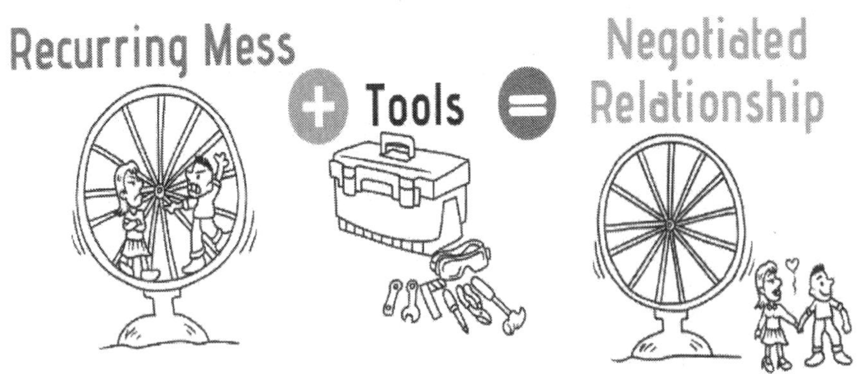

Full Acceptance of Others

Acceptance is not enough. We need **'Radical Acceptance of Others'**. To have a healthy/successful relationship, we have to start on our own side by learning how to accept another human being fully.

Being accepted, seen and valued for ourselves is one of our core needs. It's a wonderful gift to receive and one of the greatest feelings in the world: You like me exactly the way I am – you like me for myself!

But we're often unaware how much we try to change others to fit into our perspective of how they should be so that we feel safe, needed and in control of our lives.

My husband loves adventurous things, especially when it comes to things that fly and jumping off mountains. I never realized – until I decided to become completely, radically honest with myself – how I was subtly discouraging him or being less than enthusiastic about what he loves, loves, loves. I may even have organized 'an important event' or two once or twice to keep him by my side. OK, I am crawling out from under the rock of shame now…

I needed to make the decision that what he does with his free time is not up to me , that I have no say in his choice of passions and to realize that if I managed to 'contain' him I was effectively keeping him from self-actualizing. I was lucky that I grew past having my safety and security in life all deposited onto him. I grew up. I decided to fully accept him.

It's not easy to be married to someone with ADD. There are the mood swings, the love for dangerous adventure, the impulsive actions, the excitability-in-certain-trigger people's-company, the unpredictability, the addictive personality, the self-esteem hurts, the thoughts-that-tumble-from-his-mouth-unchecked-freely-hurting-me…

It's not easy. But it's what it is. I no longer accept responsibility for his messes. I don't prevent negative outcomes anymore. I speak up when thoughtless talking hurts me. When I stopped he had to take responsibility for himself and learn to manage his ADD. Which he did. But accepting his ADD needed to come first for me. I had to separate 'him' as an acceptable person from this thing he needs to deal with – even more than I have to.

Sometimes the opposite is true. Sometimes someone is trying to change us into who they need us to be.

Clara's husband is well off and from a prominent society family. He married Clara against his family's wishes, but he was madly in love with his gorgeous, sassy wife. At the same time, he was looking at a career in politics and understanding the value of connections. Now this could have gone very differently if he had accepted Clara's free spirit and let her do her art and natural healing courses in peace. Instead he used emotional blackmail and subtle references to her family to get her to comply to his family's view of what a politician's wife should be like.

"I slowly gave up 'me'. I believed in 'me' less and less. I tried hard to be what was expected of me, and I think I played the part well. I am sure no one suspected I was holding my breath waiting for my life to start.

"I was vulnerable to Sam's barely visible coercion because I felt so inferior. After all, my family is not well off. They are just ordinary people. It's not that Sam ever said anything nasty or behaved badly in any way. It was more a knowing that he was a bit ashamed of my family.

"The turning point came one day when my car stopped dead on my way to town. It was as if a dam broke inside me. I cried for what felt like hours. Finally, an acquaintance found me on the side of the road and phoned the doctor. I was quietly hushed into an expensive 'rest' facility. While I was there something clicked: I wasn't happy.

"How did I miss that? I had been pretending for so long that not being present in my own life felt normal. I kept up the happy, successful role for so long that I believed it."

We can completely give away who we are to please someone else. We may not even know who we really are!

But who is to blame for this? Is Sam the villain? He did act after all on his exterior sense of self-worth, which was tied up in being part of this successful family and in celebrating his career path. As he had a less-than-perfect internal sense of self-worth concerning who he is without his family's money and achievements, he couldn't honor it in others. But ultimately, he is not to blame. Clara willingly gave herself away in order to be accepted; to feel more worthy.

What would the outcome have been if she remained true to herself? I would say the Princess of Wales is the greatest example of what happens when one remains real and true to who you really are – you change a family, a nation, a dynasty. And if Diana could do it in the eyes of the world, against centuries-old ingrained habits, what kind of fresh breath could you bring into the lives of the people surrounding you when you decide to 'do you'?

Similarly, it wasn't my business to be my husband's adult, no matter how much I cringe when I make this kind of true confession. It always was his job to have a "No", to ask for what he wants and needs. He is responsible for negotiating his own way through our relationship.

Full acceptance of others starts with accepting ourselves.

A note of caution:

Fully accepting someone doesn't mean accepting bad behavior! It's just about finding the right language: "You're an awesome person and our relationship is very important to me. However, I need to tell you how hurt I am by your behavior."

Transforming Exercise:

1. What are you trying to change in your partner?

2. What have you allowed your partner to change?

3. What would full acceptance look like?

Before we look at what a good relationship looks and feels like, let us look at the other end first:

In a toxic relationship you feel

- Pressured

- Confused

- Guilty about not feeling good enough

- Uncomfortable around your partner

- Scared

- Humiliated

- Bad about yourself

- Trapped

- Fearful about what you say

- Mistrust

What makes a healthy relationship?

All relationships have positive and negative elements. However, a relationship that is more negative than positive is not a healthy relationship.

In a healthy relationship:

- Healthy communication consists of both partners being able to ask for what they need and willing to state what doesn't work for them in a loving but firm way.

- Both partners are encouraged and allowed to grow, as individuals and together as a couple.

- Both partners' emotional and physical needs are met. They are adults who take responsibility for getting their own needs met. They are willing to negotiate to find ways in which they can meet the other's needs.

- Validation and support is freely given and received.

- Both partners offer and receive empathy and understanding.

- True intimacy is achieved by both allowing themselves to be emotionally, physically and intellectually open and vulnerable and by materially sharing. Both feel valued intellectually, emotionally and physically. Both are willing to be real and vulnerable.

- Both parties ask for help and are able to receive it. They allow the other person to be there for them.

- Each partner is accepted for who they are. Partners don't try to change each other into what they would like them to be. Each partner shows up fully as themselves, and treats their own personal choices, needs and viewpoints with self-respect.

- Give and take occurs naturally.

- Trust is mutual and earned.

- Partners can have fun together, be playful and laugh together.

- Partners share responsibilities with mutual respect and through negotiation.

- Healthy adults in relationships have a clear sense of boundaries which they communicate clearly. They are respecting of their partner's boundaries.

- Each one's right to autonomy is encouraged and privacy is respected.

They don't need someone to complete them. They don't need to seek drama but value continuity. They accept those around them and don't try to change them into who they want them to be.

In order to achieve a healthy relationship, basic self-love and self-respect are required, even while you're continuing to grow and get healthier. Self-love and self-respect are acquired when you accept yourself, even aspects of yourself such as your sexuality and sexual orientation, and your past wrongs. This is when you're able to validate yourself rather than look at someone else for self-worth.

Healthy adults are in relationships because they choose to be, not because they need to be, and when they choose to leave a relationship because it's no longer good for them, they can do so with relative ease and not feel devastated, worthless and alone. Yes, it will suck, but healthy adults know they will work through the hurt and the loss and not be permanently devastated.

Transforming Activity (Workbook p. 56):

1. Do a self-evaluation based on the list for toxic relationships and the list for healthy relationships.

2. Decide what you don't want to allow anymore and set out how your boundaries and consequences will look.

3. Also think about what you're missing in your relationship and how you can ask for it.

Two people love each other only when they are quite capable of living without each other but choose to live with each other.

— M. Scott Peck

Chapter 30

Put Your Attention Where You Want To Go

We easily become entrenched in focusing on the negative. This is especially true if we haven't yet managed to pull ourselves out of the victim trap. From the victim perspective, life is harder because we act from perceived powerlessness.

When we're stuck there for a long time it becomes a habit to see everything from a negative viewpoint. "It's hard, it's impossible, I cannot, he has to, if only, yes but..."

We end up seeing only what we don't have and what we wish were different. We only see the problems.

The brain has a natural negativity bias, and it takes awareness to overcome it. It's what Rick Hanson calls "inclining the mind towards the positive."[28] It's really a boot camp for brains! By training ourselves to focus on the small, wonderful things in our lives, we rearrange our neurons and synapsis and grow new connections.

We can choose to establish a daily awareness of the wonderful things around us:

- The smell of a flower
- The sun shining through the leaves
- The kindness of a stranger
- The cat purring on your lap
- Rain on the roof
- Birdsong
- Puppy breath
- Beautiful music
- A hug
- A feather on your pathway

We can start a gratitude journal and write down three things we're thankful for daily.

We can find things we can do to make life better:

- Reach out to others
- Smile more
- Dance, sing, laugh
- Start a new hobby
- Plant a tree
- Visit someone in need
- Give lots of hugs
- Look for the best in people and accept them as they are
- Ask for what we need

- Expect more!

Expecting more is a powerful thing. When you expect more for yourself, your whole energy changes. You attract better people and better opportunities. You have more energy and are more effective.

When you expect more of others and believe in their capabilities, you're the wind beneath their wings, but not their rudder or steering. Having someone believing in us and encouraging us is a transforming thing. It helps us believe in ourselves! And when we believe in ourselves we conquer the world!

> Years ago, I told a mom that her daughter is super talented in pottery and that she should encourage her to keep doing it. It was only when the mom left that I realized I confused the kid with the wrong mom. I talked to the mother of one of the struggling kids. But that little girl kept coming to every holiday pottery class. And she got better and better, until her work was the best in the class. That day I unwittingly changed her life by accidentally giving her self-belief.

When you learn to not focus on the problems in your relationship or what you deem flaws in your partner, miracles happen.

It doesn't mean ignoring bad habits or negative behaviors. But it sounds different:

"Although you're struggling to rebuild your life, I know that there is a capable person inside you who can build an awesome life. I will be right beside you when you decide what you want to do."

"I know it's hard to find a job when you have a record of addiction, but you have changed your life around and I am proud of you. What have you not tried yet?"

"I sometimes still struggle to trust you, but I see that you're determined to show me how trustworthy you are. I admire that because I know it must be hard for you too."

"When you flare up at me over nothing I feel really hurt but I trust you to work on it because I believe that you don't want to carry on that way."

"I know you're not happy, but you're the only one who can look for a professional to help you cope. I cannot do this for you but you're a resourceful person, so I trust your ability to find help."

"You may think you're without choices, but you're clever and practical and all you need to do is look for a better option. I believe in you. What are some things you can do?"

By asking probing questions, being encouraging and not taking someone else's responsibility, you can change the outcome of your own life and theirs.

In order to expect more of someone in a relationship, you have to become willing to ask for more. You first become clear about what you need, then you ask and are willing to let someone show you that they can do better.

Focus on what you want in the relationship, not on what you don't want!

What is it **you** want?

If it's connection, ask for it. Stop moaning because you don't have it. And be willing to give it.

If it's to be heard, ask for it. Don't withdraw or become hurtful. And be willing to hear the other person.

If it's respect, ask for it. Respect yourself first. Don't retaliate. Give respect to the other by expecting them to show up in adult mode to your "No".

What are you putting in?

If your primary relationship (or any other relationship) is hard for you, it bears investigating what you're really putting in.

Are you moaning, criticizing, negative, critical, challenging, rebellious, spiteful and/or expecting someone else to fix you by being all things for you?

How many loving interactions, positive words, physical touch, encouragement, kindness and support do you add in?

You have to fix your side first before you even look at anyone else. Change your own attitude and see what happens.

Your **Self-Examining and Transforming Activities** are on **page 58 in your Workbook.**

Where attention goes energy flows; where intention goes energy flows!

— James Redfield

Wants And Needs

Before we can even ask for what we want and need in life, we've to know what our wants and needs are. Surprisingly many people don't know what their wants and needs are or that they are supposed to have wants and needs!

Women are especially good at pushing their own needs into oblivion and taking care of others' needs!

- If you're a people pleaser, other people's needs are more important than yours.

- If your source of self-esteem is serving others, then "bye bye" wants and needs!

- If you feel insignificant, small and invisible, you're not going to claim wants and needs for yourself.

- If you're struggling to even consider that you're of worthy of wants and needs, you're most likely looking at yourself through someone else's eyes. Whose voice do you hear in your head when you try to rise above your feelings about yourself? It's time to say "No thank you, your opinion is yours and I don't need it anymore – I am as worthy as any other human being."

This may be hard for you, but think about this: is the life you're creating for yourself not better off if you learn that it's up to you to decide and evaluate what you believe about yourself?

It will help to go back to your photo of yourself as a toddler, take a good look at the chubby cheeks, and ask: "Are you the only one born without a right to wants and needs?"

Of course you're not! You're a special, one-of-a-kind human being with every right to wants and needs, just like everyone else! So, go ahead, write down that list!

Consider the alternative: when you don't take responsibility for your own wants and needs, you're on the Hamster Wheel where someone else has to fix you and take responsibility for you!

Transforming Activity (Workbook p. 59):

1. Write a list of your wants and needs. 'Wants' are things like a puppy or a new dress, but 'needs' relate to what you need to be fulfilled versions of yourself. (No, that extra block of chocolate is still a 'want'!)

2. This list can grow and change as you change. Keep it in a place where you're regularly reminded of your responsibility to yourself: taking care of your wants and needs!

3. Hint – take another look at the chapter on *What is a healthy relationship?* to identify more healthy wants and needs.

4. Do something rewarding for yourself this week. It can be a walk in the park, listening to your favorite music, running a bubble bath, or if you habitually don't spend money on yourself, buying something for yourself. Think

for a minute – you'll know what it is when it makes you light up inside, you radiant being! Then you commit to do this for yourself regularly by scheduling your treat in your diary!

5. You go, girl, because you're so worthy!

Chapter 32

Self-Esteem 101

I did then what I knew how to do. Now that I know better, I do better.

– Maya Angelou

A positive sense of who we are smooths over our path more than anything else. It's the quality that makes you interact better with others and that spontaneously draws people to you. It's the fuel inside you that boosts you to achieve those things you want for yourself.

The opposite is true too. A lack of self-esteem presents itself in all areas of our lives.

Mark what you can identify as your problems (**Workbook p. 61**)

- Reactiveness/blow-ups

- Anxiety/stress

- People-pleasing

- Inability to be yourself – acting in a manner which you think people will approve of

- Loneliness

- Feeling powerless, which gets misdiagnosed as Depression

- Withdrawal

- Serial relationship disasters

- Under-achievement

- Over-achievement leading to burnout

- Addiction or substance abuse

- Procrastination

- Lack of assertiveness

- Body image problems

- Indecisiveness and being other-directed

- Unable to 'own' your achievements

- Feeling helpless and unable to control your life

- Feeling undeserving of being happy

- Blaming others – a victim outlook

You can determine your own self-esteem score by seeing how many of these effects currently apply to your life, and then by committing yourself to a few key exercises that will improve your self-esteem.

Wait, I feel great about myself, but I am messing up my relationships!

If you're a **high-achiever** who is **driven to succeed** you likely have **External Self-Esteem** in oodles! External self-esteem is **about what we do and achieve, not about who we are**. Although external self-esteem is useful in building our self-image and confidence, it's only when we celebrate who we are – not what we do – that we've repaired our self-image and can live as healthy adults.

Sometimes we firmly believe that we've good self-esteem. Yes, some people do truly like themselves, but often a dead giveaway of low self-esteem is how we let ourselves be treated – again and again and again.

When we have mainly external self-esteem we become

1. Either burned out by the need to overachieve, where no achievement is ever enough

or

2. Utterly paralyzed by fear of failure, which in a relationship means losing someone.

Firstly, Understanding Self-Esteem

Self-esteem is not some magical quality we have to toil for. It's a birthright, and it's something that circumstances, parenting styles and the influencing people in our life can chip away from us or enhance. A lack of a good internal sense of self is not a life sentence. It's a starting point.

Self-esteem influences how we present ourselves to the world and how we behave in relationships. It's like a window through which you view the world. If the window is clean and sparkly, the world looks brighter, but opaque glass completely obscures the world. Sometimes other people wrote letters all over your window, and you have to strip those letters off before you can see clearly.

We think of self-image as 'who we essentially are', but in an unconscious life it's made up of:

- Who we think we should be

- Who we pretend to be to please other people

- Who we wish to be

- Who we're too scared to be

- And the bit that got left over from who we're really supposed to be.

How we internalize these beliefs predicts which roles we will take on in life, which doors we choose to open and which paths we will be too scared to take.

If you wipe these other letters off your window, you can rewrite the story of where your life will go from this point forward. Although self-esteem takes time to build up, you can achieve immediate change through making a few small adjustments. Other self-esteem habits take a little more practice to settle into, but when you make celebrating yourself a daily habit you'll be amazed at where you can be six months from now! These changes will empower you to be braver through self-belief, making better choices for yourself through self-respect and attracting better opportunities through self-worth.

The Four Self-Esteem Commitments:

These four actions have the power to make you improve your sense of self, one day at a time, when you combine them with the understanding that your self-esteem deficiencies exist only because you internalized outside influences.

1. No more self-bashing – It's merely a bad habit. Stop. Yes, really just stop – every time you catch yourself. Ask people to support you by pointing out to you when you self-bash. It will not take long for you to drop the habit, especially if you say something positive instead: "I do better when I know better" or "I did the best I could and that makes me happy".

2. How you want others to see you – How you see yourself is how others see you. Now think about how you see yourself. Is that how you want others to see you? Write down a full and complete statement about how you want others to see you, stick it somewhere you can see it, and start viewing yourself that way.

Our expectation of a specific outcome shapes how we behave, which influences the way others see us. In turn, others' positive feedback cements the new belief.

Years ago, as an insecure twenty-four-year-old who couldn't reach out to others, I read this somewhere: 'How you see yourself is how others see you'. I was horrified when I recognized how filled with shame I was about my father's alcoholism. I saw myself as less than others. I didn't believe that I could be liked for myself. I either didn't speak or spoke way too fast because I was scared people would stop listening. I didn't want people to think I was unlikeable. I even avoided the tea room on the pretext that I was working, but in reality, I didn't know that I was socially acceptable. It was painful, and it was lonely. I felt like an outcast, but I did it to myself.

I decided I wanted people to see me as friendly, competent and successful as well as kind and acceptable. And so, I started acting as if I was all those things. And it got easier. And better.

Years later, when I was thirty-five years old, my mother once again told me that I am a child of the devil and would never amount to anything. This time I was empowered to say that I fought for my self-esteem, that I added it inch by inch, and that I wouldn't let her or anyone take it away from me. This habit, combined with refusing to bash myself any more, is what got me to the point that I could find it in me to say to my mother, after so many years of that specific verbal abuse: "No more!" It was the beginning of becoming whole.

3. The good points list – Make a list of your good points. If you struggle, ask your best friend to make the list for you. These can include things like being kind, a loyal friend, caring, empathetic, passionate, hard-working and funny.

Add all your achievements, your accomplishments, what you do for others, what people like about you. The list will grow as you open yourself to the awesome being you already are. Trust me!

4. Positive affirmations – Affirmations are a powerful tool that anyone can successfully apply to repair self-esteem holes.

They are self-fulfilling prophecies or beliefs that become true because we're acting as if it's already true!

How to do it:

- Write simple yet powerful messages to yourself

- Stick them where you can see them. The mirror, the toilet, the steering wheel, your screen saver...

- Repeat them out loud several times a day.

- Keep them short and positive.

- Writing affirmations is powerful, especially as part of morning pages (first thing in the morning writing) or before going to bed at night.

- Meditation changes your brainwaves to a more receptive space and is recommended for anyone who wants to experience faster positive change. You repeat your affirmations during your meditation practice for maximum effect.

It has been proven that you don't have to start out believing your own specially created affirmation for them to work. As long as you keep repeating it, your brain will start believing it until it becomes your new truth. A simple yet powerful tool, and the results are well worth the effort. (The alternative has not been working so well, has it? Nothing to lose then!)

The Law of Positivity states: "You're actively changing what you don't want in your life by replacing it with positive self-talk." You're now using positive self-talk to create a new life. When you repeat positive self-talk, you become a different person. You effectively change who you are by changing your thoughts and words. A positive conversation with your mind makes your life as positive as you want it to be.

Breaking Self-Esteem Acquiring Action into doable chunks:

Self-Worth – When we feel like we're valuable, important people.

<u>Action</u>: Do something nice for yourself. I would go and pick flowers in the garden or schedule a tea break with a friend and say, "because I am worthy". Decide what it is you want to do for yourself, say out loud "because I am worthy" and do it regularly.

<u>Affirmations:</u> I am born worthy, like everyone else. I matter.

Self-Compassion – Treating yourself with kindness, empathy and understanding.

Understanding your imperfect perfect humanness can change how you see yourself and feel about yourself. Decide to start treating yourself like you treat your best friend.

Action: Write down a list of how you can treat yourself better, as you do for those you love.

Affirmation: I am my own best friend. I am kind to myself.

Self-Feeling – Learning that it's possible to accept and express our feelings.

Action: Find a safe person or a support group you can express your feelings to. When you become ready, those people will come on your path. Your part is to reach out. Find names for your feelings using a **feelings chart. (Workbook p. 47)**

Affirmation: I have a right to my feelings.

Self-Acceptance – Accepting ourselves in entirety, the good points and the points we like less.

Action: Self-acceptance is a decision more than anything else. It's understanding that being human comes with the tendency to make mistakes until we know better. It's accepting that we could only do what we've been taught growing up, and if we were not equipped with tools, that is how it is.

Affirmations: I am fully acceptable. I accept all of me.

Self-Focus – The goal of self-focus is to be the master of our lives; to put ourselves first in our own queue.

Action: When you have not taken responsibility for your happiness for so long, you now bring your attention back to yourself each time you find yourself saying: "Yes but he..." or "She should..." You use the words "I can..." or "I choose to..."

Consider a challenging situation in your life and apply this principle.

<u>Affirmations:</u> I steer my own boat. I am first in my own queue.

Self-Guidance – Trusting our own guidance and judgment.

Self-guidance is to trust our ability to guide ourselves in a healthy way. When we have not had healthy role models, or if we've lost faith in our own ability to guide ourselves, or others, we've to learn to trust ourselves first of all.

<u>Action:</u> I stop asking people for input or approval every time. I review what I really want and take steps to make it happen.

<u>Affirmations:</u> I trust my own judgment. I determine where I want to go in life. I decide how my days are going to be.

Self-Care – Taking responsibility for one's own well-being.

<u>Action:</u> Make a list: In which ways can I take better care of myself? Decide on the three most important things to do and schedule those in your diary. Take action, book that holiday, make the doctor's appointment, get that massage, speak up for yourself, ask for what you need, use your voice…

<u>Affirmations:</u> I take great care of myself because I am worth it. I deserve joy. I can have fun.

Self-Respect – Self-respect is the base from which we make better decisions.

<u>Action:</u> Find a self-respecting person and think what they would do in your situation. Emulate their behavior until it feels natural. Self-respect feels great and once you know how great a feeling it is, you won't need to fake it anymore. You'll start choosing self-respecting words and actions naturally.

<u>Affirmations:</u> I respect myself. I am worth more.

Self-Determination – The goal of self-determination is to feel that we're empowered.

When I focus on the fact that I am an adult and not a helpless child, I step into my power.

Action: What empowers me? Make a list of where you gave up your right to choose. Decide what you want to put into action.

Affirmations: I am an adult with free choice. I decide what I like and dislike. I have a voice.

Self-Love – Self-love is the ability to love ourselves as we are.

Am I re-parenting myself best or do I look to others to make me happy?

Action: Today I decide that I like myself exactly the way I am. I make a solemn declaration that henceforth I will treat myself like my own best friend.

Affirmations: I completely and truly love and accept myself. I am lovable. I am the only one who can be me. I do 'me' best. I like myself.

And then you decide to be different:

Here is how **Ingrid** did it:

"For many years I suffered from low self-esteem. During therapy I worked on my self-esteem. After a time, I decided I needed to practice what I had learnt.

"I was invited to a wedding far from my home. The only people I would know at the wedding were the groom and the groom's parents. The guests would be spending the weekend as they came from all over the country and overseas. I shared a chalet with a family I had not met before. We all got along well. On my drive there I did have a few misgivings but knew that there would be a lot of people there in the same boat as me.

"The Friday evening everyone got together for a welcome party. I met lots of new people and made connections. I had made the decision that I would involve myself in all the activities. The wedding was great. I talked to different people, danced with a group of people and had a really pleasant evening.

"The best part of the weekend was near the end of the wedding. I was standing outside as it was so warm. A lady started chatting and said she wished she was as brave as I was: to go away for a weekend, by myself, and still have a great time. I realized it was about showing up and being yourself."

It wasn't easy for Ingrid, and she had to push herself to do things differently. As the weekend progressed she continuously built on her self-esteem by seeing the results of her bravery. By taking action and trying new things we discover a powerful self-esteem tool: new activities and purposely different behavior build self-esteem!

How we feel about ourselves may be the simplest definition of self-esteem. To love yourself, value yourself and like yourself is to have self-esteem. Self-esteem is a big job but taking these steps will get you there. Remember that where you put your attention is where you'll go!

There are some powerful and life-changing **activities** for you in the **Workbook (p. 61 to 64)**. They have the power to change your life forever in the best possible way.

If you want a more structured approach with help and individualized support on your road, this Self-Esteem Course (http://bit.ly/2GvPmLs) will speed up your journey.

You're a beautiful and beloved individual.
It's good to be you.
We will love you no matter what you do,
as long as you're you.

— M. Scott Peck

33.1 Understanding Boundaries And Having A No

Complete your **Self-Evaluating Exercise** in your **Workbook (p. 65)** before you continue reading.

I will never know which part of my story I could have been spared if I had had an inkling about loving myself enough to set boundaries. I don't believe in 'what if' or 'I should have' kind of thinking and have no intention to do any kind of self-bashing. We do the best we can with whatever tools we were issued. We follow our unconscious learning until life events wake us up from sleepwalking our way through 'hard', to 'harder', to 'traumatized'. Then we get ready to set boundaries!

What if we feel controlled and powerless to change it?

We tend to view abuse as being violent and angry.

But it has more to do with someone's basic inability to accept your "No" and your boundaries. They will stop at nothing to get their way! They will figure out which buttons to push to get the reaction they are set on, and they will keep on using it as long as it's effective.

The basic inability of another *to accept* your way and your wishes stems from a deep psychological desire to 'not feel less' or 'not feel wrong'. Their fragile sense of self is so grounded in the safety margins they set up for themselves that they have to get those inside their circle to comply, so they can feel safe and in control. Feeling in control is the clear driving need for them.

Those trapped in this sphere of control wrongly assume that they are not powerful. Instead, **the controller is perfect at creating the illusion of control and power.** It's an illusion because no human has the capability to control another human. In the end you still have the capability to decide what you will allow and what you won't. Some may want to say they have no control over finances or access to alternative shelter, but that is still a choice. To trade your internal happiness for a meal and a bed is a choice, as much as it was a choice not to have a clear "No" the first time you were disrespected.

It serves us well to remember that not making a choice is still a choice. And when that is the choice we make – to not make a choice – then we cannot hold anyone responsible for that but ourselves.

In *The Road Less Travelled*[29] M. Scott Peck reminds us that making a decision is an inevitable, albeit scary part of growing up:

Many never take any of these potential enormous leaps, and consequently many do not ever really grow up at all.

– M. Scott Peck

Victor Frankl[30] gives us the ultimate example of a human being's capability to retain the ultimate control over self. He realized that everything could be taken from him, but that he alone had control over his thoughts, his attitude and his outlook. In the face of the most debilitating circumstances he survived the Holocaust to be an inspiration for millions.

> *When we're no longer able to change a situation,*
> *we're challenged to change ourselves.*
> *Everything can be taken from a man but one thing:*
> *the last of the human freedoms –*
> *to choose one's attitude in any given set*
> *of circumstances, to choose one's own way.*
>
> – Victor Frankl

Giving up our right to having a viewpoint, a preference and a boundary is a choice. If we do give up those birthrights, the onus remains on us to find out why and to find a way to change it – gracefully!

For women the problem of **having a right to a "No"** is even bigger than for men. Although we're not as stereotyped as we were a generation ago, many of us are still subliminally brought up to be sweet and obliging. "Be nice, darling. Nasty girls don't have friends. Willful women don't get husbands!" The right to have wants and needs was not taught to us.

Transforming Activity 1:

Ask yourself: what were the messages I was taught as a child? How was I controlled into being compliant?

How our parents resolved conflicts would also be a great influencer on our lives. Their examples and communication styles would be repeated in their parenting styles, and we would unconsciously learn to emulate them or to respond in a certain way to please them. These learned behaviors are deeply ingrained, but once discovered can be adapted to a more conscious style of communicating.

Transforming Exercise 2:

Reflect on how your parents communicated with each other. What was good? How did they quarrel? Did they resolve their issues? How respectfully did they communicate with you? Were you allowed a "No"?

The optimal way of resolving conflict is to have two mature adults allowing each other to have different opinions while feeling free to voice disagreement in a respectful manner. In this respectful space a solution would be negotiated. They would follow this communication style with their children too, and children would be given more and more choice as they become older.

However, we're more often witnesses to other kinds of conflicts:

- The screaming match. Someone will be blaming, someone will be justifying or retaliating.

- The dominance-through-anger-and-volume attack.

- The suffer-in-silence mope.

- The withdrawal game.

- Moralizing and guilting people into submission in the nicest way possible.

- Passive aggressiveness. The air is contaminated with antagonism and malevolence, but with no awareness of suppressed anger and hurt.

Conflict in itself is not bad. It's a necessary tool in the evolution of relationships. If there is no conflict it simply means that one individual is not a fully self-expressing partner – one part of the relationship is not contributing but following. Conflict can be meaningfully resolved in a respectful manner. It's important that we know this in order to become willing to establish boundaries in our lives:

Difference in opinion is not a problem, but necessary when we choose to build a strong relationship based on mutual respect.

What exactly is a boundary?

(Recommended book, even if you think you have 'strong limits', like I did! *Boundaries,*[31] by John Townsend and Henry Cloud.)

The most important principle in boundary setting is this:

You don't have a boundary
if you don't have a consequence!

Having boundaries may be a problem for some, but having consequences we're willing to stick to is what most people struggle with. We're so often subliminally ruled by our unconscious fear of abandonment that we will not act on our consequences even if we've conveyed them. We're prone to have a compelling urge to jump in and fix the problem by any means available to us. We're very likely to use the method most likely to get us a feeling of 'closeness'.

For some women it may be resorting to tears, because that usually generates a remorseful partner.

For others it's an urge to repair the relationship with sex. That would explain amazing 'make-up sex', in which both parties feel a surge of connection and belonging – one of our undeniable basic human needs.

Some need long conversations with repeated assurances of the other's commitment and undying love and repentance. Some will overcompensate and cook favorite meals or buy expensive gifts.

Hence, the consequence is not acted on. **Our unconscious need to repair connection** remains bigger than our need to have a better relationship, until the unconscious need becomes visible to ourselves. Only then can we establish mindful consequences which will enable us to have – for the first time – a deeply connected relationship based on mutual respect of each other's boundaries; not based on a mutual desire for connection by filling each other's unmet needs.

The formative years are crucial for us to learn how to accept and set boundaries.

It's only in the teenage years, usually after twelve years of age when puberty starts,[32] that the human brain gets the chemicals it needs to challenge our primary caregivers, to examine their actions and to make up our own minds about the validity of other people's opinions. For those lucky enough to be brought up during this stage with an emphasis on decision-making and learning consequences, consequence setting and accepting becomes easier.

If you were not treated as respectfully, with loving, firm boundaries, you'll not have a reference system for setting boundaries or accepting them. (Furthermore, it's worth noting that children who grew up without boundaries don't have a sense of safety in the world because they inherently don't believe their parents loved them enough to set boundaries.)

What size a consequence should be is the next problem for the person who has not been allowed to learn boundary setting in their formative years.

We who are unskilled in 'consequence setting' start by asking: "What should the appropriate consequence be?"

However, we can do much harm if we have an 'all or nothing' attitude. We tend to think in black or white: "If you don't do this I am moving out". Between no consequence or too high a consequence, our relationships have zero chance to grow.

We have to learn that consequences come in variable sizes, and we can choose a consequence we can live with. If your consequence is "I am moving out", the emotional cost may be so high for you that you won't stick to your boundaries. This is more doable: "Our relationship is important to me, but I cannot work on it by myself. I am moving into the spare bedroom until you're willing to work with me on repairing our relationship by seeing a couple's counselor. It's your choice to work on the relationship or not. I cannot force you. But I can take better care of myself." It can be even smaller: "My love, I care for you deeply, but picking up your clothes is not part of my job description. I am going to let you be your own adult so if you don't have clean clothes it's your own business and your own choice."

A consequence can be a molehill, not a mountain.

I recommend practicing consequences on people who are not that dear to you. The serviceman, the contractor, the lady behind the till taking your order – those are the people you practice on: "I want to be clear that although you're the most skilled person, I will take my business elsewhere if my order is not complete by the agreed date. Is that acceptable to you?" or "As it's vital for my business that you're on time, I am only prepared to sign the contract if there is a penalty clause built into it for late delivery. If you choose not to add the clause I fully respect that but then I choose not to accept your quote."

Notice the lower boundary in the second example, with no loss of firmness or self-respect. Also know that a firm but pleasant tone is essential. A harsh tone does not belong with setting an adult boundary.

Free choice for the other is the magical requirement:

When you desire to be in a relationship in which you are treated with love, respect and kindness, it's vital that you communicate in a way that respects the other as an adult with free choice.

"I need assurances from you, so I can feel safe until I have learned to trust you again, but I cannot force you. It's completely up to you to be willing to support me that way or not."

"I am no longer willing to stay in a room when you shout at me. I am willing to talk things through calmly, but I cannot force you to communicate in a calmer way. You're the only one who can decide how you choose to communicate. But I can take better care of myself by not participating in screaming matches anymore."

"It's not possible for me to work on our relationship when you withdraw. It saddens me but as an adult you're the only one who can decide if you want to work through our problems or withdraw. Please let me know when you're ready to work on our relationship, but until then I have my own life and interests that I will concentrate on."

Boundaries are NOT ultimatums!

In an ultimatum there is no free choice. When there is free choice, it's setting a boundary.

When you set a boundary as an ultimatum you're likely to have a spiteful/child/victim/retaliatory reaction on the receiving end. When you do it without guilting, blaming or judging but with leaving free choice to the other, you have a much bigger possibility of getting an adult response. Mind your tone and your body language, and you're on the road to success.

The only thing remaining now is for you to **take responsibility** for your own emotional health and for your part in the relationship. In becoming willing to voice your wants, your needs, your preferences and your non-negotiables, you're controlling the only person you're able to control – yourself!

You may encounter resistance, and you may need to learn how to have a conversation in which you feel heard, but we will get to that when we get to *Difficult Conversations.*

Pick Your Battles!

When you first get over your unconscious resistance to setting boundaries, and find out the benefits of setting them, you may get a little carried away...

It's an excellent idea to write down your new boundaries, list them in order of importance, and to differentiate between 'boundaries' and 'wants'. **Boundaries** include actions or habits you cannot live without or are not willing to endure ever again.

Wants are things you ideally would like to see happen. They will be a great improvement to your life but will not ultimately influence the quality of your life in a make-or-break way.

As you can imagine, it would be a little overwhelming to be presented with a list of twelve non-negotiables and thirty wants all at once. You're likely to end up with a partner who feels extremely judged, criticized and rejected.

The reaction can be that it's impossible to satisfy you or that your partner feels like a total failure when presented with such a long list. This will result in a person in defensive mode or in withdrawal.

Focus on the one or two things most important to you, work on those, and when you have successfully addressed those, you'll notice that the less important things on your list get resolved by themselves.

33.2. Non-Negotiables

Here are a few facts regarding non-negotiables:

- Everyone should have them. If you don't have them you may be a people pleaser, have self-esteem impairments or have traumatic abandonment fears.

- You're the only one who can determine your non-negotiables.

- You can change your non-negotiables as you grow in self-trust and self-direction, or as circumstances dictate.

- No one has to give in to your non-negotiables. People have free choice over their own compliance or not. You can only ask and gracefully decide on your next course of action if someone chooses not to respect what is dear to you.

- Nor do you have to give in to someone else's non-negotiables if they are things you're not able to give or feel uncomfortable with.

- Non-negotiables are not a battle of wills. They are asking and receiving or moving on to your next course of action.

You have an absolute right to express what you are under no circumstances ever to do or willing to endure. After so many years I am done with having a husband who drinks. My sober alcoholic husband is very clear that I will never, ever do that to myself again. I feel absolutely no guilt or responsibility to him here, just utter and complete love for myself. And also forget about me ever doing bungee jumping...

No one can determine *your* non-negotiables or tell you what they should or should not be. That is your job and your responsibility to yourself!

Transforming Activity (Workbook p. 66):

Write down your non-negotiables: It helps to think about what would make you feel respected, heard, valued and safe in a relationship.

33.3. Avoidance of Conflict

Some people will do anything to avoid conflict. Do you recognize yourself in any of these? **(Workbook p. 66)**

- Having no self-confidence.

- Being valued for being a nice girl 'who doesn't make trouble'.

- Your role in the family was 'peacekeeper'.

- You don't know that you have a right to a voice.

- You were not encouraged to have an opinion or choices growing up.

- You were continuously shamed, so you gave up.

- Your abandonment issues make you believe that you'll be deserted if you speak up.

- You're acutely aware of your peacekeeper role in your relationship and find great value in being that person for your partner. You feel a little superiority in being able to do this thing, so he can be the undisputed king of his castle.

Jessie tells us how she lost her voice: "We were four girls who shared a room. My older sisters took whatever they wanted and without thought disrespected me and my stuff. If I complained my parents just said that I must take better care of my stuff. It was impossible. I had nowhere that was just mine. I was shamed, not helped."

Elaine was the oldest of four: "My parents blamed me for whatever my siblings did or didn't do. I felt invisible and learned to completely disappear into books until I learned how to physically disappear. I would sign up for after school classes and offered to stay on and help the teachers, so I wouldn't have to go home and be responsible for everyone else. At least the teachers appreciated me. Years later I realized how I was hurting my marriage by still disappearing and looking for appreciation elsewhere."

There are many ways for people to avoid conflict:

My husband used to go outside and smoke rather than talk to me. I had no clue that something had frustrated, irritated or hurt him.

Someone else may pour another drink in order to handle the feelings they cannot verbalize. (He did that one too!)

Addiction will serve as an avoidance of conflict – whether it's playing bridge or watching back-to-back series or being in other people's business, watching sports obsessively or whatever excuse you find legitimate.

Simply agreeing with everything is avoidance of conflict too. So is people-pleasing.

Transforming Activity:

How do you disappear/avoid conflict?

- Do you pretend not to notice?

- Do you make yourself guilty?

- Do you deny your feelings?

- Do you suppress your feelings until you explode?

- Do you withdraw into something else? What?

- Are you relentlessly cheerful?

- Any other way?

Do words like 'negotiate', 'discussion' and 'disagreement' have negative connotations for you?

Another important issue to look at is the emotional meaning you attach to words like 'confrontation', 'conflict' and 'disagreement'.

'Confrontation' can change to "I value my contribution enough to state it in a clear, non-combative way".

'Conflict' can be changed to 'healthy discussion' in order to reach an agreement".

'Disagreement' can be changed to 'two healthy individuals acknowledging each other's right to a different opinion'.

'Argument' can change to 'working towards a negotiation'.

'Fighting' can change to 'engagement through mutual respectful communication'.

By now you have worked through your triggers, through your influencers growing up, and you have identified unresolved hurts. You understand the importance of taking your own responsibility. Part of this responsibility is to claim your voice in a fair, non blaming, non-judgmental, non-guilting way.

Your contribution strengthens your relationship. It's true that two heads are better than one. Your unique viewpoint is needed to make it truly an equal union of two individuals.

It's also unfair to your partner and your relationship if you don't step into your own adult, and instead retreat into punishing withdrawal or passive aggressiveness. That remains true even if your partner is not used to you having views and input, and even if your partner sees his role as parenting or saving you. The opposite is true if your partner is the avoidant.

Sooner or later we learn to put on our big girl panties, take responsibility for our own happiness and be self-directed. That is when we have to learn how to have difficult conversations.

Up next!

But first, **re-evaluate your answers to the questions in your Workbook (p. 65).** You may want to add or change something after reading the chapter.

Chapter 34

Difficult Conversations

Difficult conversations are… DIFFICULT!

- Until you learn how to do it

- Until you see that it works

- Until you value yourself so much that you have no choice but to trust your rights and your voice and your worthiness.

There are steps to follow if you want to have:

- Effective communication,

- A way to resolve disputes, and

- A way to have your needs met.

But first it will be helpful if you learn how to get a bit of distance, dial down the fast fire emotional response and buy yourself a bit of time to get objectivity.

Withdrawal vs. Detachment

Withdrawal is what we don't want to do to ourselves under any circumstances. We already know that is not how we get what we want and need, nor does it benefit us in any way. It's the way we harm ourselves the most!

So, what is detachment then?

It's putting a distance between you and the emotion, to reflect objectively on what just happened. It means you're not emotionally in the fray, but you have not walked away. You're willing to keep communicating as soon as you have sorted out your triggers and chosen your response.

You detach from your triggered emotions, not from the person or the relationship.

The Child – Adult – Parent Trap (or Transactional Analysis)

The first thing to do before we can have a transforming conversation, is to check in which state we are.

- **Child Mode:** Feeling persecuted, feeling set upon, feeling trapped, feeling powerless, emotionally over-reactive, rebellious, retaliatory, blaming, spiteful, manipulating through tears and helplessness.

- **Parent Mode:** Judgmental, scolding, lecturing, finger-wagging, manipulation through guilting and shaming, feeling superior, hyper-critical.

- **Adult Mode:** Emotional reactions are worked through, a course of action has been chosen, responsibility has been taken for own happiness and for own part in problem situations. Self-respect and mutual respect are the driving forces.

Effective or Destructive Communication Styles

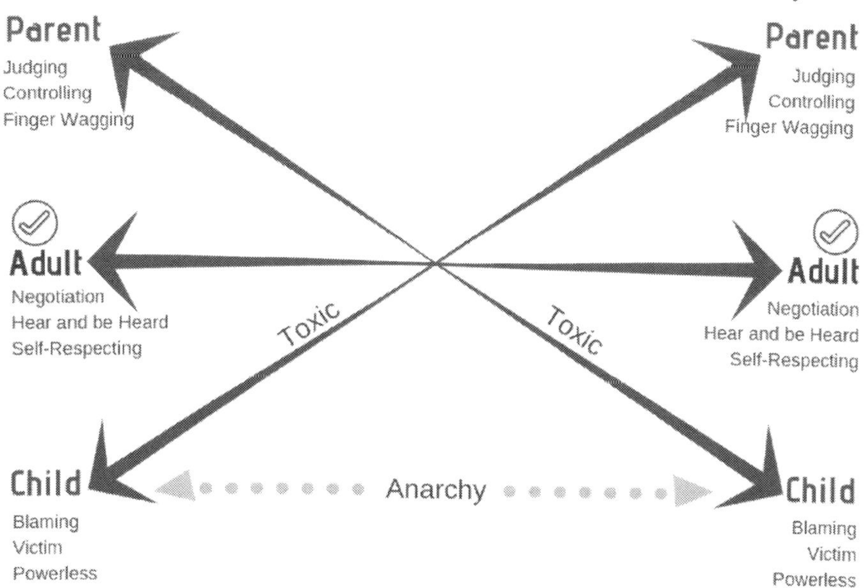

In **Child Mode** the pervasive feelings are helplessness and powerlessness. This is an anxious, defensive and oftentimes confrontational state – you're in victim mode. If you have strong Child in you, your helplessness and dependency will trigger Parent Mode in someone who has strong Parent in them.

In **Parent Mode**, the pervasive need is to change someone else. You feel morally obliged to scold, blame, shame and criticize someone else until they do what you have decided is best for them. You use words like 'have to', 'ought to' and 'should'. You don't trust someone to take care of themselves and feel it's your job.

In Child Mode and in Parent Mode your needs are **fear-based**, as you're motivated by your own fears of abandonment, rejection and vulnerability. You can move fluidly between the two modes, depending on the trigger.

The worst state is when both parties are in Child Mode – that stage resembling two toddlers kicking, screaming, pulling each other's hair and crying hysterically. That is where the Hamster Wheel relationship often deteriorates to: two out-of-control people punishing each other.

In Adult Mode, over-reactions have been mindfully replaced by logical reasoning. You have released triggered emotions, you are self-regulating, you are taking total responsibility for your own happiness and for your own part in the mess. You're coming from a place of equality and you're respecting the other.

This stage takes determination to get to and practice to stay in. Once you experience self-empowered behavior and find out how great self-respecting action feels, you'll want to stay there more and more. You'll see that communication is much more effective in Adult Mode. Your "No" is "No". Your stance is firm. Your voice is even. Your state is calm and sure. There is nothing morally superior or helpless, only great self-love and clarity regarding what you want in life, and what you won't allow.

(For more information, read Eric Berne's book, on Transactional Analysis, *The Games People Play.*)[33]

Defensive Habits

We all get ourselves grown up by adapting various defensive habits. The ones that are effective and that feel good will stick. We will identify with them and say, "It's just who I am". We will cling to them and defend them as they helped us feel normal and in control. In times of stress we will automatically want to revert to them, so becoming aware of them is vital. These defensive habits distract us from working through our problems and we don't need them anymore – once we've fully stepped into our true role: that of being an empowered, self-directed adult with choices.

Transforming Activity:

Which of the following habits are yours?

1. Learned Helplessness – you get results by being helpless or you have given up your belief that you're capable.

2. Innocence at all costs – defend, defend, defend. It's immediate and always the first and only reaction as someone has not learned it's OK to mess up.

3. Minimizing – if you make it not important, you cannot be guilty, right?

4. Rationalizing – talk in endless circles about how you cannot possibly be guilty until you find a good reason you cannot be guilty which you stick to relentlessly.

5. Intellectualizing -- making it an intellectual issue which you can park in a safe little box makes you feel a measure of control.

6. Moralizing and criticizing – a mortal fear of being wrong.

7. Withdrawal -- I cannot be hurt when I avoid my feelings.

8. Emotional shut down when overwhelmed – a leftover habit from a powerless childhood.

9. Negativity – if I expect nothing I cannot be disappointed.

10. Shifting responsibility – my lack of self-esteem doesn't allow me to take responsibility.

11. Perfection and over-controlling – I need a feeling of safety in the world.

12. All-or-nothing attitude – I don't believe that I have a voice with which to communicate and negotiate. My needs will never be important.

13. Over-analyzing and ruminating --by putting my attention there I don't need to focus on my lack of tools to handle the present.

14. Generalizing – you don't have insight into your own inner turmoil so you make the entire world responsible for your happiness by not stating specific pain points clearly. You cannot identify them, so you say, "you always" or "you never".

15. Being in other people's business – it's keeping me so busy that I have an excellent excuse not to focus on my own problems.

16. Over-Doing Anything – it very successfully distracts me.

17. Busyness – I am too busy to think about my problems. I am important because I am 'a busy person'.

18. Addiction – different kinds of addiction replace the need for coping tools and fill up the gaping hole inside us.

Be aware that others are ensconced in these patterns too and that these patterns can interfere in the negotiation process. However, your job is not to be someone's counselor or fixer – your job is to take care of yourself by communicating clearly-defined boundaries in a loving, not rejecting way.

The other person must do with their defense systems what they choose or choose not to do!

The Difficult Conversation Process – Step By Step

Step 1: Stop. Don't react. Don't withdraw. Excuse yourself. You can say you need a few minutes to gather your thoughts. Or that nature is calling. Sometimes we need to remove ourselves physically from a person through distance, as their presence is compelling us to people-please. Their anger or their guilting may be subconsciously triggering our 'comply' response and the amygdala needs to be switched off in order for reason to prevail. Sometimes I step back a foot or two and mentally remind myself, "I stop here, you stop over there – your thoughts or wants cannot jump inside me unless I let them." Any or all of these tricks are usually enough to get me back into my own body and back to being self-directed.

Step 2: Ask: "What is this all about?"

First switch off the following habits:

- Making it about yourself – Perhaps he cannot show up for a date because he is in an emergency meeting, not because he doesn't want to be with you. Once you automatically know in your bones you're such an awesome person that there can't be any possible reason why anybody wouldn't want to spend time with you, your rejection trigger of 'making it about yourself' is switched off. Then you also know that if someone doesn't want to be with you, it's because you two are not suited in his eyes. It happens. It's not because you're undesirable or unworthy; it's only his preferences.

- Decide not to generalize, guilt, shame, blame, judge or justify. These things have no place in adult conversations, because they put you into either a victim or parenting position which will have victim or parenting responses. When you don't generalize, guilt, shame, blame, judge or justify the mud is cleared from the pool and you can see your way to an adult conversation. These six habits are the 'Terrible Six' and keep you locked into the Hamster Wheel of Never-Ending Same Old Arguments.

"What is this all about?" is followed by "What is the hurt?"

"What is this about?" answers this: Why am I reactive?/Why is he reactive? The answer will be something like this: "I am triggered because he talked over me."

"What is the hurt?" helps us get to the root so we can convey our feeling in a vulnerable way to the other: "I am hurt because I feel invisible when you talk over me."

Once you understand that you're reactive because you're hurting and once you have identified the exact hurt, and you're back and in charge – you have effectively taken control back from your subconscious. Now you can be reasonable and logical. Above all, you can be effective if you drop the Terrible Six.

'**Why** is he reactive?' is not your hamsters and your zoo; you just need to understand that if he is reactive, he is reacting because he has his own unresolved business. You let him have his own business to decide what he wants to do with it – if he wants to do anything with it – in his own time.

Step 3: Take your own responsibility. Acknowledge your part, at the very least to yourself. It's not terrible to be wrong; it's terrible not to know you're wrong! And not to even examine the possibility is unrealistic. Any relationship consists of two people who will both be right, and both be wrong. It's life, but shifting blame robs you of your power and puts someone else in the driver's seat.

This is not self-bashing yourself into helplessness! Self-bashing is not based in self-love. It's a helpless, victim state.

However, when you without hesitation examine how you caused it, you know which action sequence to follow. "I realize I didn't tell you that I dislike it if you don't tell me when you won't show up. I feel unimportant to you if you do that. I will not wait for you next time if you don't let me know in time." There you go – you had no boundaries, so the problem keeps on coming back – Hamster Wheel style!

Do you see the difference?

An error doesn't become a mistake until you refuse to correct it.

- Orlando A. Batista

Step 4: Check your own body language and listen to your tone as you speak. Passive aggressiveness and hurt in particular are impossible to hide, but a condescending outlook, judgmental stance and rejecting reaction will show in your body language or your tone as well. You can say the sweetest thing, but if you do it in a tart tone, your real feelings will be picked up. You don't need to hold back on your words when it's delivered in adult style without the emotionally triggering weight of the Terrible Six. When you claim your voice and are real about how you feel deep inside, your body language and tone will not need to convey your frustrations and repressed aggression.

Step 5: By now your triggered responses should have abated by taking these steps involving logic. Now is the time to decide on your chosen course of action by doing this inventory:

- See if you have to apologize first. This is not a form of self-bashing, it's taking back your power because you recognize how you can do better next time by changing your own behavior: Maybe you didn't set a boundary with a consequence; maybe you didn't ask for what you want and need or maybe you didn't show up in vulnerability. It could be you were the one who was out of line.

- See if you set proper boundaries with consequences or if you failed to convey these convincingly. Or do you have a habit of not sticking with consequences?

- Find the lesson and decide how you can get better results next time.

- Set a boundary and a consequence you're committed to sticking to.

- Refuse to take another adult's consequences. You'll take those consequences forever onto yourself if you don't give them back. If you want a great relationship, allow him to grow up and have his own consequences.

Step 6: Communicate clearly. Don't expect your partner to mind-read, except if he is a psychic! "Yes, but he should know", is shifting your responsibility to 'talk' onto someone else. People only know how we want to be treated and what we will not tolerate if we tell them!

Step 7: Difficult conversations targets our 'End Goal'. When we're clear about what we want to achieve, we can have conversations about it. Do I just want to be heard and respected? Is it hurting myself to keep living with an alcoholic? Will I most definitely not be second fiddle to the entire world, in other words, do I want to feel important to my partner? Or do I simply need help with preparing the meal as I am so tired and stressed out?

It's time for the difficult conversation...

It's not because things are difficult that we don't dare;
it's because we don't dare that they are difficult.

-- Seneca

The Difficult Conversation – Step-by-Step

1. Validate the importance of the other person or the relationship. Express appreciation and speak in a warm tone.

2. Admit his right to his feelings or his views even if you don't agree with him.

3. Keep the Terrible Six out of the action: No Generalizing, Guilting, Shaming, Blaming, Judging or Justifying.

4. Get a buy-in. Ask if it's a good time. Don't assume that it's a good time because you feel like it. When you ask input on a good time for a conversation, you'll have more cooperation.

5. State how you feel. Noooo, not: "I feel you're an idiot." State your feelings: "I feel hurt/ I feel invisible/ I feel rejected/I feel abandoned." This will only work if you're willing to be vulnerable.

6. Example: "I feel hurt when you…"

7. Choose your battles. Only tackle one problem at a time, so carefully decide which issue is the most important to you. When you sort out the big ones – feeling unimportant, feeling not heard, feeling not wanted, feeling rejected, feeling less – dirty socks on the floor somehow lose their importance. You stop fighting about everything-and-nothing when you work through the big ones.

8. State your boundary (NO Terrible Six please!) and your appropriate consequence. Remember to choose your consequence carefully. Not so small that it's not effective at all, but no need for Mount Everest in every case.

9. Stop speaking. If you monopolize the conversation you're bullying the other into submission and being

disrespectful of their input. Not giving someone else the opportunity to be heard is not communication. It's you in either parenting mode, in which you believe your input is superior, or it's you in fear mode. Through continuously speaking, those in fear mode try to manipulate the other into what they want, or to prevent them from taking the feared course of action.

10. Really listen. Listening only happens when you stop speaking. If you truly want to step off the Hamster Wheel, now is your chance, as every human being wants to be heard. During the listening stage, be aware of three things:

- Don't formulate a response. That is not listening – that is defending.

- Don't interrupt or tell someone what they should feel or think – that is parenting.

- Don't project – that is your own insecurities hijacking the conversation.

- Don't decide for the other what they are feeling or saying or meaning – ask them, they are right there. Deciding for them and dumping your interpretations into the conversation is emotional hijacking.

11. It's not enough to say, "I hear you." You have to believe that another person has a right to an opinion which you may not like or agree with. They still have that right, no matter what you think or want, and just by respecting the other person as a separate person with separate wants, you start a whole new way of communicating. When the other person truly feels heard, reactivity gets neutralized and you have two adults in the room. And you have exactly the same right in return.

12. What if you're faced with a non-talker? You can still talk. Keep it brief. Ask for what you need. Tell him how not communicating makes you feel unconnected or invisible or…

13. Continue by giving each other time to speak, listen properly, respond mindfully. In explosive situations one of two techniques work well. Take a look at an Imago conversation on YouTube or try this tip from Mark Waldman, Neuropsychologist:[34]

Limit dialogue to one sentence

lasting ten seconds or less.

Each participant has to carefully

consider their few words, which helps

to take away the Terrible Six, and

focus on the most important problem.

This has been proven to resolve most

impossible communications in

less than five minutes!

Step 8: Stick to your consequences. Your actions and words are inconsequential if you don't stick to your consequences – a totally wasted effort. You're heaping flaming coals on your own head and will keep getting the same unwanted result if you don't decide to step off and do things differently by letting the other person have the consequences you're not willing to take away for them anymore.

Resistance

Not everyone is ready. Not everyone is adult enough. Some people have too much unresolved childhood hurt and reactivity in them to be able to come to the table. It may be ugly; it may be uncomfortable to watch someone puking their feelings onto you. But that is their own baggage to carry. You can simply love them, re-evaluate their role in your life, and adjust to what you need to do next.

Keep a place in your life for them. Most people grow continuously. You don't need to feel resentment or project their feelings onto and into your behavior. You can just be yourself – open and with no attitude next time you see them.

This becomes possible once you see someone else as an adult, separate from yourself, with free choice to comply or not, and with his own preferences, outlooks and choices. This is when you don't make it about your own unresolved hurts and needs, but believe in your own adult capacity.

Those people in our lives who can respect our
Boundaries will love our wills, our opinions,
our separateness. Those who can't respect our boundaries are
telling us that they don't love
our no. They only love our yes, our compliance.

– Henry Cloud, John Townsend[35]

Chapter 35

Conclusion: Do You Ever Give Up On A Relationship?

We tend to either give up too fast and for the wrong reasons or stay in relationships way past the point of deserving. But how, oh how, to get into balance, when we either cannot trust our instincts or are a bundle of too-fast-overreactions?

It's a process...

- First, we learn to love and respect ourselves.

- We learn to give ourselves time before we react.

- We drop a lot of debilitating habits like blaming, judging, guilting and making it about ourselves.

- We let adults be adults and have their own consequences.

- We learn to be vulnerable and show people who we are.

- We become willing to ask for what we need to thrive.

- We learn how to set boundaries with consequences and have difficult conversations.

Then we give people the time and the opportunity to 'show up better'.

'Show up Better'

When we ask to be respected and treated with love and appreciation, we have to let someone have the opportunity to show whether they are willing to be a better partner in a relationship or not. Like you, your partner also has to learn new tools and step into his own adult shoes, with a new set of behaviors and outlooks.

The willingness to learn new skills, be flexible, apply oneself when it gets hard and to renegotiate a new relationship are miracles that can only happen if you ask of your partner to show up better.

You do this by being vulnerable, by exposing your hurts and by asking for what you need in a self-respecting stance. You do this by having the difficult conversation clarifying what you'll never tolerate again while affirming that you value the relationship and your partner.

'Show up better' doesn't mean you try to change someone. It means your partner takes responsibility for his part in the Hamster Wheel and is willing to work to make it better. Just like you're willing to show up better.

Hopelessly-in-love addiction

This is when the connection with/to the other person feels so right that you don't care if there is a truckload of disasters in your relationship. The only thing of importance to you is that you feel healed and completed enough by the relationship. You won't want to do any work on your relationship because you'll fear abandonment and loss too much to stir up anything.

You'll most likely not make it to the end of this book!

Here is where that kind of thinking doesn't work: Hopelessly-in-love addiction is giving up your adult powers of self-determination and self-directedness to a codependent relationship. Because that is what love-addiction really is.

It will keep working until one, or both, grows up or becomes fed-up with being one another's adult. This is when the Hamster Wheel arguments start all over again.

Working slowly through this book and the exercises is an excellent way of ensuring you never end up in such a relationship again. Instead, as an empowered adult, you can now choose to be in an ever-better relationship: one between two self-respecting adults.

When does it really not work?

You may still not be respected and heard even though you have done your part. You could have learned to use the tools in this book and you may have pushed through your fears and become vulnerable and real and self-respecting, but your relationship could still be struggling. In that case I would suggest that you commit yourself to seeing a couple's counselor before you think about separating. Very often we struggle because we're unable to see our own blind spots. Sometimes both parties need a neutral interpreter, and both having the tools learned in this book will make the professional's job so much easier.

The Four Horsemen:

John Gottman[36] describes the sure signs of a relationship doomed for failure in his excellent book *Why Marriages Succeed or Fail: And How You Can Make Yours Last*. After years of research he found the following to be sure signs that a marriage is not in going to make it. I would hope that when you have reached the end of this book those threats don't exist in your relationship anymore:

- Criticism

- Contempt

- Defensiveness

- Stonewalling (withdrawing)

My ultimate list of what to take into consideration:

1. If you're in physical danger, get help and support for a fast and safe exit.

2. If you're the only one working on the relationship, it's time to seriously reconsider your options. Relationships have hope if two people give it their all. Your relationship will still get better if only you work on it, but it's up to you to decide if that is good enough for you.

3. Not having chemistry can happen between two people who have had too much trauma between them. But it can be rebuilt better than ever, so that is no reason to leave a marriage without giving it a good go. Chemistry can reappear when both parties feel a mutual respect, are willing to hear each other, can have fun together, and can be real and vulnerable with each other. If you've never had chemistry it may be because one or both was emotionally switched off or because you have been primed to only find dangerous relationships exciting.

4. There are many relationship-building skills a trained professional can help you with in a few sessions. You can get help with the practical things we need to do to rebuild a relationship:

- Have daily time for each other,

- Concentrate on bringing hugs, loving touch and warm tone back into your relationship,

- Go on dates, do new things together,

- Reintroduce laughter and fun.

5. Be aware that sometimes someone will not have the capacity to give emotional connection, have rational and intelligent conversations, or be a caring individual. These may be your personal preferences and needs, and it's not to say that things may not change in this individual's life when life pushes them to dig deep. You have to decide if you want to wait around and for how long. A lack of capacity needs realistic consideration and evaluation without judgment. Accepting to remain in such a situation is a choice for you to make, or not.

6. If you're making a decision in times of high emotion, you're likely not ready for that decision. Nor will you be in an adult state in which you can make an evaluated, contemplated and rational decision. You need to determine if you're in the Hurt Cascade or the Self-Respect Cascade:

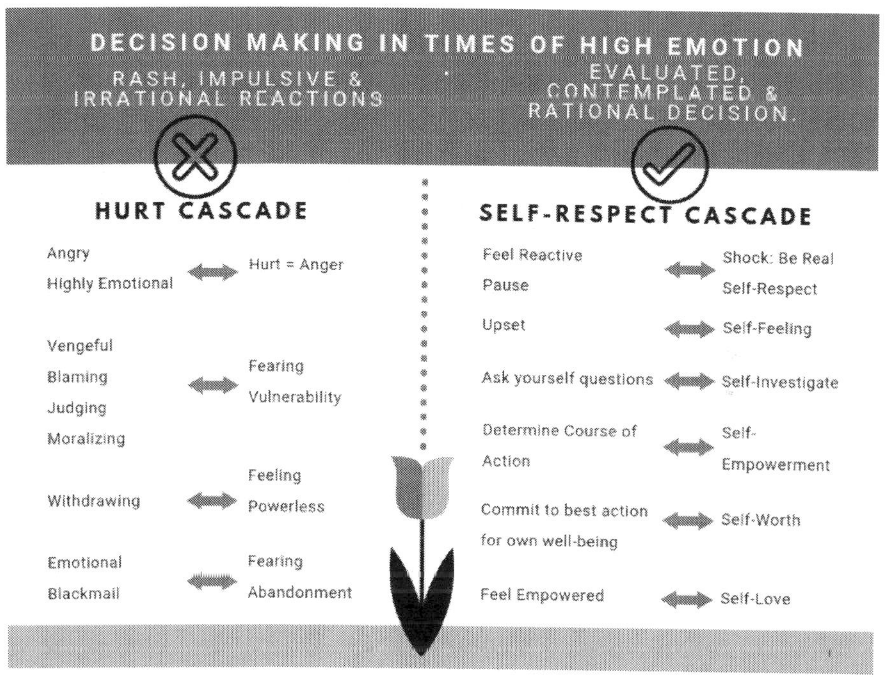

In the Hurt Cascade you're highly emotional, vengeful, blaming, judging, moralizing and/or withdrawing. In the Self-Respect Cascade you know that you're worth more and desire peace and a loving and kind partner who is willing to engage with you respectfully. You're not overly emotional or angry. You're hurting but willing to convey that in a calm and rational way. You have a certainty and calmness that you're on the right path. You're willing to walk away and experience the loss because you desire a better relationship more than you need the dysfunctional relationship. You're not denying the loss or refusing to feel those feelings; you're acknowledging them but are empowered by self-love to change your life.

7. Know that it starts with YOU. If you're waiting for someone else to change or for magic to hit you from the sky, you'll only prolong your own suffering. Your life changes when you look at yourself as an adult with choices and rights and a voice. You can learn to differentiate between being lazy, stuck, scared or giving up. You'll do well to notice that you yourself may be stuck in negative habits. You have to recognize, on the other hand, that this may just not be the time or the place for this relationship; not right now as it is.

And that only *you* can do. But now you can do it with your new skills and new tools.

Your last **Transforming Exercise** is on **page 69 in your Workbook.**

A Love Letter

I didn't thank my husband in the beginning. I needed you to read through this first to understand that I couldn't be who I am today if I didn't fully accept the trials life brought into my road.

And for every challenge and hardship I am truly thankful. It enabled me to grow into someone who is capable of being real and happy every day. In the midst of hard things, I know that I am still good in my core.

And I can help others from a place of experience with no judgment and total acceptance.

We walked a long road, but it started with both of us changing things in our own lives. We both became whole individuals. I am very proud of him for conquering his addiction. I am very proud of him for thriving, despite ADD, by working diligently at establishing coping strategies.

As the two of us started on our journey to rebuild our marriage, he could have given up. He could have decided that the shame was too much or that he wanted to keep denying that ADD has a major impact on one's life. He could have decided that it would be easier to move on to a new fun relationship than do the hard work of rebuilding a mess.

But he didn't. And day by day, month by month, we've been rebuilding our relationship to be better than it ever was. This is the kind of relationship worth working for, and worth fighting for.

And I couldn't have done it on my own. Nor could I have written this book of hope for hopeless relationships. I would also not be able to help my clients from a place of inner knowledge that it can be done.

Thank you, Love.

Acknowledgements

The Anonymous Ones – I couldn't have written one word of this book without the brave, vulnerable, amazing group of people who have been part of the support groups I facilitated over the last eight years. You trusted me, you opened up to me, you taught me about your challenges, you were willing to try a new approach and you persevered. Your changed lives are my biggest reward. Thank you for showing up, in all possible ways. So much love to each and every one of you.

Dom – You're my starfish. If you need throwing back into the ocean, I am here.

Jenetta Barry – Sometimes we're lucky enough to have people in our life who change its direction in a positive way. You're one of my saving people, and I am fortunate to call you friend, mentor, confidante and soul sister. I benefited from your support and your example – in joy and in grief. How you transformed the devastating loss of your daughter to suicide at sixteen has been a big inspiration and lesson to me. Countless others have since been supported and guided in their loss through your work as The Grief Coach. Thank you, my friend, I made it, thanks in no small part to your example, your friendship and your willingness to be unpopular by letting me see it as it really is.

Sarah Farquharson – I trusted you with my well-being like I have never been willing to trust anyone before. With loving kindness, true support and so much space for my grief, hurting and healing journey you supported me on my first steps to a new life. I am eternally grateful to you

319

Sally C. – Because you took a chance on reaching out to someone you barely knew you're touching countless lives without even knowing it. Everyone who reads this book participates in a process started by your generous act of paying it forward. Because you saw someone in need.

Karen McKenzie – Sometimes one word gently, daringly, carefully said is all that is needed.

Simone Descoins – You're the exception to my psychologist rule. You made a difference.

Angela – You helped me process and release my feelings. With your gentle spirit you use healing intuition and a special kind of Angela-magic.

SPS Mastermind Community – Your selfless sharing of knowledge, inspiration, hand-holding, butt-kicking and ruthless rejection of anything but the best for my book pushed me forward and upward. Thank you so much!

Beta Reader Team and Launch Team – You're the quiet soldiers who made the army march! Thank you for helping me help others. Your dedication and support is heart-warming and I deeply appreciate your time; the most valuable thing anyone can give to another.

Vivian Blac – Thank you for the use of your poem *'cause I'm your mother*. It tells it like it really feels. You have a gift and thank you for sharing.

Russell Barnes – My copy editor and friend. RIP; life is short of a wordsmith, thinker and moral human being.
Karen Edwards Photography – Thank you, miracle worker!
Illustrations – Hasto Bagas Himawan, Aryo Pamungkas & Tina Wijesiri
Editor – Joy Sephton of Just eMagine
Cover – Heidi Sutherlin

About the Author

Drawing heavily on her professional experiences and her own transformational process, Louise VN Liebenberg, Life Coach, Counselor, Rescuer-Of-Abandoned-Cats and Road-Trip-Lover shares her no-nonsense, practical approach to mindful and constructive involvement in one's own life.

She lays out a fresh approach to relationship building and shares the outlook-changing, no-nonsense self-empowerment tools that are needed in a step by step way.

She combines her experience as a stained glass and ceramics artist with her passion for empowering others to achieve their goals by offering different ways to view challenges and to approach life.

A multitude of stray cats share their small-village-life with her and her husband.

THANK YOU FOR READING THIS BOOK!

Before you go, please help out if you enjoyed this book by posting an honest review of it on Amazon or Goodreads.

By cutting out the middleman, I can connect directly with you, my reader. But without the huge marketing resources of the big publishing houses I rely on you to get the word out to other people who may also enjoy this book.

I know your time is precious, but it will help me improve this book and my future adventures. It will only take a few minutes to do a sentence or two. Reviews are the lifeblood that enables Amazon to show a book to more readers.

Your experience will be valuable to others looking for support and your feedback will be warmly received.

Upcoming Books And Other Life-Changing Stuff

The next book in the series will be for men:

NO MORE Series *Book 2.*

Hamster Wheel Relationships for Men:
A Manual For Mastering Relationships

Other upcoming titles:

- Hamster Wheel Relationships for Couples: A Step By Step Commitment to Fulfilling Relationships

- Hamster Wheel Relationships for Families: A Step By Step Process In Establishing Healthy Family Communication

- Hamster Wheel Relationships In The Workplace: A Step By Step Structure for Successful Professional Relationships

- No More Codependency

- The Self-Esteem Solution

Sign up to be notified about release dates and special launch offers by visiting:

https://landing.mailerlite.com/webforms/landing/y9b0z4

Also for preferential prices before books are made available to the public.

(I never spam readers; I am too busy writing my next book!)

Facebook Hamster Book Supporter Group– where you can stay informed and involved, vote on covers and features, plus get sneak peaks into the book writing process. Your input determines what I write next!

https://www.facebook.com/groups/hamsterwheelbooksupporters/

- **Workbook PDF**. Download it and print it. In order to maximize the effectiveness of this book, it is recommended that you work through the questions, exercises and activities of the Workbook with honesty and willingness to find hidden truths. This process will speed up and cement your transformation.

- **EBook** – How To Get the Connection And Support You Always Wanted.

- **Check List** – Am I Contributing to a Mess or a Success through my Communication Style?

- **Cheat Sheet** – The 4 Best Self-Esteem Boosting Hacks.

- List of Highly Recommended And Helpful Books to read.

Download your Workbook and all your FREE bonuses here:

https://www.subscribepage.com/l3f9k7_workbook

Website: www.i-nfinitepotential.com

YouTube:

https://www.youtube.com/channel/UCfBh-dMQF4QG1liJqSCp7aQ

Facebook Support Group (Please use as an answer to your security question the code word: choice**)**

https://www.facebook.com/groups/hamsterwheelrelationships/

References

[1] Ackerman, Robert J. Perfect *Daughters: Adult daughters of alcoholics. 2nd ed.* Deerfield Beach FL: Health Publications Inc., 2002. 158 – 196.

[2] Cates, John C., Cummings, Jennifer. Recovering our children. A handbook for parents of young people in early recovery. New York: Writers Club Press, 2003.

[3] Rostocki, Adam. *Cure Back Pain Forever: A Primer to Mindbody Medicine.* 3rd ed. United States: Independently Published, 2017. 31 – 51.

[4] Meinecke, Margaret. Web:
http://instituteforattachment.ong/adult-attachment-disorder-cognitive-therapy-with-attachment-challenged-adults/

[5] Blac, Vivian. *I write no color pictures.* United States, Amazon Digital Services, 2017.

[6] Hegstrom, Paul. Broken children, grown-up pain: Understanding the effects of our wounded past. Kansas City: Beacon Hill Press, 2006.

[7] Vandervoort, Debra, Rokach, Ami. *Social Behaviour and Personality.* Web: Social Behavior and Personality: an international journal, Volume 31, Number 7, 2003, pp. 675-685(11), 2003

[8] Rodman, Karen. Web: http://theneurotypical.com/posttraumatic_relationship_syndrome.html

[9] Schwartz, Lisa. The Comprehensive Resource Model: Effective therapeutic techniques for the healing of complex trauma (Explorations in Mental Health). New York: Routledge, 2017.

[10] Ortner, Nick. The tapping solution: A revolutionary system for stress-free living. Carlsbad CA: Hay House, 2013.

[11] Barry, Jenetta. A Handful of Keys for Grief Relief. www.jenettabarry.com

[12] McGraw, Phillip C. *Self Matters: Creating Your Life from the Inside Out.* New York: Simon & Schuster, 2001.

13 World Service Organization. Adult Children: Alcoholic/Dysfunctional Families. 5th ed. Torrance CA, 2006.

14 Casey, Karen. *Codependence and the Power of Detachment.* San Francisco: Conari Press, 2008.

15 Hanson, Rick. Buddha's Brain: The Practical Neuroscience of Happiness, Love & Wisdom. Oakland: New Harbinger Publications, 2009. 96 – 106.

16 http://www.wisebrain.org/slidesets/SlidesPaperTiger.pdf

17 Hinrichs, Jonathan, M.S, DeFife, Jared, Westen, Drew. *Personality Subtypes in Adolescent and Adult Children of Alcoholics: A Two Part Study.* Web: https://www.ncbi.nlm.nih.gov/pmc/articles/PMC3143015/

18 Klipin, Judy. Life Lessons for The Adult Child: Transforming A Challenging Childhood. Johannesburg: Penguin, 2010. 10 - 22.

19 Dayton, Tian. Emotional Sobriety. From Relationship Trauma to Resilience and Balance. Deerfield Beach Fl.: Health Communications Inc., 2007.

20 Bradberry, Travis, Greaves, Jean. *Emotional Intelligence 2.0.* San Diego: Talentsmart, 2009.

21 Hanson, Rick. Buddha's brain: *The Practical Neuroscience of Happiness, Love & Wisdom.* Oakland: New Harbinger Publications, 2009. 96 – 106.

22 Bradberry, Travis, Greaves, Jean. *Emotional Intelligence 2.0.* San Diego: Talentsmart, 2009.

23 Hoff, Benjamin. *The Tao of the Poo.* London: Mandarin Paperbacks, 1982. 27.

24 https://comprehensiveresourcemodel.com/crm-the-comprehensive resource-model/

25 Osansky, Eric M. Hashimoto's Triggers: Eliminate Your Thyroid Disease by Finding and Removing Your Specific Autoimmune Triggers. United States: Amazon Digital Services, 2018. 74.

26 Brown, Cathy. ACT: Align-Connect-Transform: Discovering the 5 Foolproof Steps to Create the Life You Want. United States: Amazon Digital Services, 2017.

27 Osansky, Eric M. Hashimoto's Triggers: Eliminate Your Thyroid Disease by Finding and Removing Your Specific Autoimmune Triggers. United States: Amazon Digital Services, 2018. 74.

28 http://www.rickhanson.net/overcoming-negativity-bias/

29 Peck, M. Scott. The Road Less Traveled: A New Psychology of Love, Traditional Values and Spiritual Growth. Great Britain: Hutchinson & Co. 1983.

30 Frankl, Victor E. *Man's Search for Meaning.* 1992 ed. London: Rider, 1992.

[31] Cloud, Henry, Townsend, John. *Boundaries: When to Say Yes, When To Say No To Take Control Of Your Life.* Michigan: Zondervan Publishing House, 1992.

[32] Hegstrom, Paul. Broken Children, Grown-Up Pain: Understanding the Effects of Our Wounded Past. Kansas City: Beacon Hill Press, 2006.

[33] Berne, Eric. Games people play: *The Basic Handbook of Transactional Analysis.* New York: Random House, 1964.

[34] Newberg, Andrew, Waldman, Mark Robert. *Words Can Change Your Brain.* New York: Penguin, 2012.

[35] Cloud, Henry, Townsend, John. *Boundaries: When to Say Yes, When to Say No To Take Control Of Your Life.* Michigan: Zondervan Publishing House, 1992. 108.

[36] Gottman, John. Why Marriages Succeed or Fail: And How You Can Make Yours Last. New York: Bloomsbury, 2012.